"I read t
disappo.
In this book, one can feel the love of monastic life and the
feminine side to it."

— Aquinata Böckmann, OSB

"Would that we had more examples of disciplined imagination
to bring theology and history to life! This 'lost' dialogue, which
sounds just like Pope Gregory and Deacon Peter, gets past and
present into a kind of call-and-response. It's as if Gregory's
202-year successor, with his concern that women's gifts to the
church be celebrated and rights in the church be increased,
were to turn his hand to Scholastica's story. The book is
instructive—and lots of fun."

— Patrick Henry, retired executive director of the
Collegeville Institute for Ecumenical and Cultural
Research and author of *Benedictine Options:
Learning to Live from the Sons and Daughters of
Saints Benedict and Scholastica*

"It is an excellent idea by Carmel Posa, SGS, to use her profound
knowledge of sacred Scripture, monastic theology, and history
to finally give a voice to this hitherto marginalized female
'rule interpreter' by means of a hagiographical narrative and
the method of 'disciplined imagination'! What an eye-opener
and what a precious contribution to a deeper understanding of
the role of women in the history of Christian monasticism."

— Manuela Scheiba, OSB, St. Gertrud's Abbey,
Alexanderdorf, Germany; associate professor of
monastic theology, St. Anselm, Rome, Italy

"Despite the lack of historical evidence surrounding her, St. Scholastica is a 'treasure that prevails.' Balancing both creative and disciplined imagination, Carmel Posa's *The 'Lost' Dialogue of Gregory the Great* enables Scholastica to emerge from the shadows to shine, instruct, and inspire. Carmel tells a credible tale of one woman's agency and Spirit-inspired leadership—a prototype for all women who have been silenced and rendered invisible in the Christian and monastic tradition."

— Patty Fawkner, SGS, is the former leader of the Sisters of the Good Samaritan of the Order of St. Benedict

"This book uses 'disciplined imagination,' a deep knowledge of the language and themes of the Bible and early medieval sacred biography, and an appreciation of the overwhelming power of love in the Benedictine tradition to create an imagined biography of St. Scholastica. The biography is all the more powerful for its prioritizing of the 'truth surrounding the holiness of women' over simple facts or surviving documented evidence. This book transports the ancient genre of hagiography seamlessly into the twenty-first century and demonstrates that a hagiographical reconstruction is a particularly useful technique for recovering women's lives. This 'lost life' of Scholastica is a highly original study that is both completely modern and completely medieval in its technique and spirit. Perfect for reading in short extracts or in one sitting, this book is a rare treasure."

— Elizabeth Freeman, senior lecturer in medieval European history, University of Tasmania

The "Lost" Dialogue of Gregory the Great

The Life of St. Scholastica

Carmel Posa, SGS

Foreword by
Michael Casey, OCSO

LITURGICAL PRESS

Collegeville, Minnesota

litpress.org

2	3	4	5	6	7	8	9

Library of Congress Cataloging-in-Publication Data

Names: Posa, Carmel, author. | Casey, Michael, 1942– writer of foreword.
Title: The "lost" Dialogue of Gregory the Great : the life of St. Scholastica / Carmel Posa, SGS ; foreword by Michael Casey, OCSO.
Description: Collegeville, Minnesota : Liturgical Press, [2024] | Includes bibliographical references. | Summary: "In The 'Lost' Dialogue of Gregory the Great, Carmel Posa, SGS, applies a "disciplined imagination" and the ancient hagiographical method to recover the missing life and voice of St. Scholastica of Nursia. Drawing on a wide range of scholarship, including Gregory the Great's four famous dialogues, biblical models, and the Rule of Benedict, Posa follows a technique similarly used by Saint Gregory himself to create an account of Scholastica's life"— Provided by publisher.
Identifiers: LCCN 2024000945 (print) | LCCN 2024000946 (ebook) | ISBN 9798400800535 (trade paperback) | ISBN 9798400800542 (epub)
Subjects: LCSH: Scholastica, Saint, active 6th century. | Benedict, Saint, Abbot of Monte Cassino—Family. | Christian women saints—Italy—Biography. | BISAC: RELIGION / Christianity / Saints & Sainthood | RELIGION / Monasticism
Classification: LCC BR1720.S27 P67 2024 (print) | LCC BR1720.S27 (ebook) | DDC 270.2092 [B]—dc23/eng/20240209
LC record available at https://lccn.loc.gov/2024000945
LC ebook record available at https://lccn.loc.gov/2024000946

For my Good Samaritan Sisters,
Strong, faithful, and inspiring women of God.

Contents

Foreword

I have recently read Peter Seewald's two-volume biography of Pope Benedict XVI.[1] Even enriched by a wealth of material in the public domain, interviews with more than a hundred people, a team of assistants, and many exchanges with Pope Benedict himself, there are many matters that are not discussed. The author often had to make judgments on what is relevant to the picture he wishes to present—which is not without elements of advocacy. At the end of more than a thousand pages, it may well be that a reader feels bereft of information on particular areas about which there is no data, or which the author has considered outside his scope. As a result, readers will, inevitably, finish the volumes with further questions and will attempt to fill the gaps from their own imaginations, perhaps projecting much of themselves in so doing.

Those who wrote in the ancient genre of hagiography, or sacred biography,[2] never had the resources enjoyed by modern authors—a few oral or maybe written accounts and

---

[1] Peter Seewald, *Benedict XVI: A Life*, Vol. 1, *Youth in Nazi Germany to the Second Vatican Council 1927–1965*, trans. Dinah Livingstone (London: Bloomsbury Continuum, 2020); Vol. 2, *Professor and Prefect to Pope and Pope Emeritus 1966–Present*, trans. Dinah Livingstone (London: Bloomsbury Continuum, 2021).

[2] See Thomas J. Heffernan, *Sacred Biography: Saints and Their Biographers in the Middle Ages* (New York: Oxford University Press, 1988).

some local legends, if the person were particularly famous. These "sources," although often quite sparse, provided the elements from which the saints' lives were constructed. Part of the hagiographer's skill consisted in processing these bare data into a full-blooded life, drawing on accepted precedents, filling out missing details with recognized tropes, and even imagining what might have taken place. All this was done with the understanding that the person being described was a saint and, therefore, would have acted in all circumstances as a saint was believed to act.

Although in later centuries lives were written with a view to facilitating the process of canonization, the primary purpose served by hagiography was the edification of the reader; to intensify this process, the hagiographer had no scruples about exaggerating the beneficent impact of the saint, since this was done with the noble intention of improving the morals of the readers and safeguarding them from harmful opinions. Anything that might have revealed any kind of limitation in the saint was quietly left aside. Since it was solitary and exceptional virtue that was being celebrated, any potential mentors or rivals were relegated to the sidelines. The saints were considered to have arrived at high virtue through their own talents and efforts; what others contributed was always regarded as secondary.

In the case of St. Benedict, as is clear from a sequential reading of the Rule, personal and monastic development took place over the years. Part of this may be derived from concluding that he followed his own advice and immersed himself more broadly in the writings of tradition, which would have provided him with some counterpoint to the rather rigid framework he borrowed from the *Rule of the Master*. The picture of the abbot which he presents in chapter 64 is clearly indebted to the *Rule of St. Augustine*, and is much more humane and pastoral than what he had written earlier in chapter 2. The later chapters place much more emphasis on love, good zeal, and intentionality than the sometimes harsh prescriptions found at the beginning of the Rule. Perhaps this is why Terrence Kardong, OSB, suggests that we read the Rule backwards.[3]

Benedict had never led a cenobitic life, "under a rule and an abbot." When he reluctantly left his solitude and assumed the role of abbot at Vicovaro, his severity was too much for his monks, so they tried to poison him (*Dial.* III, 4). Perhaps he learned something from this. In his later dealings with disciples, he appreciated the importance of codifying the obligations of monastic life, and so he adopted and modified an existing rule, the *Rule of the Master*. Even with a stable regulatory framework, difficulties occurred and, following the example of the Master, he was obliged to make provision for the punishment and excommunication of aberrant monks (RB 23–30). In succeeding centuries, however, these chapters have not won general acceptance; they have been observed, at most, only sporadically.

What all this suggests is that, during his lifetime, Benedict had much to learn, much to relearn, and much to unlearn. This gives rise to the question of whether he had help in circumventing his blind spots and growing in maturity. Did he have some form of pastoral and personal supervision? If the answer is positive, then a not-unlikely candidate for this role would be his sister Scholastica.

Sister Carmel Posa has used a "disciplined imagination" to fill out the picture of Scholastica and to present her as a formidable exponent of spiritual and monastic values, but also as a support—and perhaps as a subtle mentor—to her famous brother. This is not done lightly. The author of these

[3] Terrence G. Kardong, *Benedict Backwards: Reading the Rule in the Twenty-First Century* (Collegeville, MN: Liturgical Press, 2017).

pages has followed a technique similar to that used by St. Gregory himself, and has drawn on a wide range of monastic sources to create a readable and credible account of Scholastica's life.

Perhaps in the distant future there will be those who will quote from these pages, assuming that they also come from the pen of Gregory the Great.

Michael Casey, OCSO

Introduction

I remember reading Gregory the Great's *Life of St. Benedict* early in my religious life. I found myself fascinated, not only by the story itself, with its powerful portrayal of a journey of faith, its notable and extraordinary miracles, and its rich and impressive words of wisdom, but also by the actual style of the writing. It was Adalbert de Vogüé's commentary on the text that demonstrated to me the brilliance of Gregory's style and the importance of this ancient and un-familiar genre (hagiography) for the writing of saints' lives, not only in terms of our understanding of history, but also as an attractive and popular medium to effectively transmit and strengthen faith.[1] Yet, what also struck me, so many years ago, was the fact that Benedict's sister played such an important, yet marginal role in this wonderfully evoca-tive story.

We are only informed of Scholastica's existence in the final chapters of Gregory's tale, and yet it is here we learn that the spiritual development of the hero of the whole story has not progressed to the extent to which that of his own sister had advanced. Gregory poignantly tells us that Scholastica achieved a more effective relationship with God through her prayers than did her brother through his

---

[1] See Adalbert de Vogüé, Gregory the Great, *The Life of Saint Bene-dict*, trans. Hilary Costello and Eoin de Bhaldraithe (Petersham, MA: St. Bede's Publications, 1993).

adherence to law or rules, and this was the case simply because "she loved more."[2] Yet, in vain do we search for stories of how this extraordinary woman achieved such a level of holiness, in spite of the fact that she has come down to us as a revered saint within the Benedictine tradition, and is so often depicted in artistic representations alongside her brother in the famous "thunderstorm story" of Gregory's *Dialogues*.[3]

It wasn't until I came across a small chapter devoted to Scholastica, in a volume which described the contributions of saintly monastic women throughout history, that I started to think more seriously about this mysterious and beloved woman of my tradition. Mary Richard Boo and Joan Braun's small chapter in this book allowed Scholastica to begin to "emerge from the shadows" of history for me.[4] Indeed, these writers sparked my curiosity even further, as it seemed well nigh impossible to assert anything concrete about the historical Scholastica at all. Like Boo and Braun, I too wanted to "glance back over the preceding sixty years of Scholastica's life," before her famous meeting with Blessed Benedict, "to consider what is not literally stated but is unquestionably clear: saints are not made overnight nor during the course of a single downpour, however precipitous their conversions may sometimes seem."[5]

---

[2] *Dial.* II.XXXIII.5 (125). All references to Gregory's second *Dialogue* will be drawn from *The Life of St. Benedict by Gregory the Great*, trans. Terrence G. Kardong (Collegeville, MN: Liturgical Press, 2009), unless otherwise indicated.

[3] *Dial.* II.XXXIII.2-5 (123–25). The story is included below.

[4] See Mary Richard Boo and Joan M. Braun, "Emerging from the Shadows: St. Scholastica," in *Medieval Women Monastics: Wisdom's Wellsprings*, ed. Miriam Schmitt and Linda Kulzer (Collegeville, MN: Liturgical Press, 1996), 1–11.

[5] Boo and Braun, 2–3.

Boo and Braun attempted a fuller picture of Scholastica, drawing mostly from pious traditions, liturgical calendars, lectionaries, lessons, homilies, medieval *vitae*, hymns, poems, and frescos which have come down to us through the ages. They even present us with the scholarly arguments for and against Scholastica's historicity, all of which still leave us with more questions than tangible insights into the life of this esteemed and holy woman. In spite of these attempts, it appeared to me that Scholastica still remained very much "relegated to an existence somewhere between myth and reality."[6]

My own academic interests have always been in the field of monastic history and spirituality, where attempts to address the often-ignored voices and lives of women, and their significance, has grown markedly over the last thirty to forty years. This corrective movement continues to undo the injustice done to women over the centuries, and provides a more balanced picture, particularly in terms of the rich contributions and influence of women throughout Christian history. This present work centers on the recovery of what appears to me as the missing hagiographical life of St. Scholastica from Gregory the Great's four famous *Dialogues.*

The first three of Gregory's *Dialogues* praise the virtues and lives of the saints of Italy; in the fourth he discusses the immortality of the soul. In the typical hagiographical style of the time, these *Dialogues* present a justification for belief in the saints. Highly symbolic, dramatic, and at times fantastical, this hagiographical form aims primarily to present the saints as images of Christ (*imitatio Christi*) in order to edify and encourage the reader to emulation and praise.[7]

---

[6] Boo and Braun, 1.

[7] For a general introduction to hagiography, see James T. Palmer, *Early Medieval Hagiography* (Leeds, UK: Arc Humanities Press, 2018),

Sandwiched between the first and third of Gregory's *Dialogues* on these lives of saints—the vast majority of whom are male, and most of them clerics—is the *Life of St. Benedict*. Here Gregory gives only scant detail concerning the sister who, although not attested to in the *Dialogues* themselves, the tradition claims was Benedict's twin, Scholastica.[8]

Interestingly, the other women of the *Dialogues* are positioned mostly to enhance the depiction of holiness of the male heroes of the stories.[9] These women often take the traditional position of carnal tempter, by way of marking the path of either perdition or holiness for the "man of God."[10] As hapless victims of the devil's wiles, they serve as markers between the power of evil and the power of holiness.[11] They are also positioned so as to elicit miracles from the holy man, or to prove his gift of prophecy,[12] or to demonstrate his selfless service of others.[13] Nevertheless, there are a few exceptions to this pattern as, for example, in the case of the saintly virgin, Gregoria. Here she runs away from home to live a consecrated life devoted to God. But it soon becomes clear that Gregoria seems to be included

---

particularly chapter 1, "Making Saints (Up)," 15–39.

[8] As Boo and Braun suggest, "Whether this designation alludes to actual birth or to the unity of spirit that traditionally binds twins, or to both, is hardly significant." See "Emerging from the Shadows: St. Scholastica," 6.

[9] For example, Benedict's female housekeeper in *Dial.* II.I.1-3 (2), and the mother of Boniface, Bishop of Ferentino, in *Dial.* I.9 (40). I have used the following translation of the *Dialogue* I, III and IV: *Saint Gregory the Great: Dialogues on the Miracles of the Italian Fathers*, The Fathers of the Church, Vol. 39, trans. Odo John Zimmerman (New York: Ex Fontibus, 2016).

[10] See *Dial.* I.4 (17); II.II.2 (13); III. 7 (120); *Dial.* III.16 (142).

[11] See *Dial.* I.4 and 10 (18, 42).

[12] See *Dial.* I.9 and 10 (40, 48).

[13] See *Dial.* III.1 and 17 (112, 145).

because of her relationship to the holy man Isaac, whose function is to protect her in her vocation. Neither her reasons for choosing to live a consecrated life, nor the effects of this choice on the world around her, are ever described in any detail.[14] Indeed, the women of Gregory's *Dialogues* rarely appear as the central characters.[15]

In *Dialogue* I, we do have an example of another woman who, like Scholastica, bests the holiness of the central male character. In this story, it is again through the power of love that a woman undoes the will of a holy man.[16] This love, as in the story of Scholastica, seems to be the overarching virtue by which women gain a position of holiness in Gregory's stories of saintly male heroes.

It is not until we get to the fourth *Dialogue* that Gregory includes women among the saintly men of Italy to any significant or numerical degree. Only after Scholastica's inclusion in the second *Dialogue* do we hear of the eschatological visionary activity and miraculous work of holy women alongside those of men.[17]

[14] See *Dial.* III.14 (130).

[15] The unnamed woman of Spoleto is perhaps a further exception to this rule. She alone stands out as both a miracle worker and an inspiration to other women to live holy lives. See *Dial.* III.21 (152).

[16] Recalling the story of Jesus and the Syrophoenician woman of Mark 7:24-37, an unnamed and tragic mother of the first *Dialogue*, carrying her dead child, is given a central role through her maternal love to waylay the humble monk, Libertinus of Fondi. He is impelled against his better judgment to help her. See *Dial.* I.2 (11). Here it is not law as in the case of Scholastica and Benedict, but male humility, that is no match for the power of female love.

[17] See for example, Galla, who takes on religious life and is marked out as exemplary on her own merits in *Dial.* IV.14 (205ff.); the famous miracle-working recluse Herundo and her disciple Redempta, as well as her disciple Romula in *Dial.* IV.16 (208ff.); Gregory's own holy aunt, Tarsilla, and her two sisters in *Dial.* IV.17 (210ff.); and little Musa, the sister of Probus in *Dial.* IV.18 (211ff.); all of whom confirm the afterlife through their visionary activity.

In the closing chapters of the second *Dialogue* there are two very famous and highly significant episodes which include Scholastica. Although she does seem to take center stage in these stories, this achievement does not immediately result in her gaining prominence in the story itself. She remains on the margins of a tale that aims at establishing the centrality of her brother's holiness.

Gregory, in the midst of explaining why saints don't always get what they desire, tells his conversation partner, Peter the Deacon, that Scholastica was dedicated to God from childhood, and that she, having her own "cell" somewhere near Benedict's Monte Cassino monastery, used to meet often with her brother for conversation.[18] Gregory relates the famous "thunderstorm" story about the last of these meetings:

> 2. His sister, Scholastica, who was consecrated to almighty God from her childhood, used to come to see him [Benedict] once a year. The man of God would come down to visit her in a house owned by the monastery not far from the gate. One year she came as usual, and her venerable brother came down to her with some disciples. They spent the whole day in praise of God and pious conversation. When night shadows were already falling, they took a meal together. The hour grew late and they still sat conversing of holy things. Then his sister, the consecrated woman (nun), asked him, saying, "I beg you, do not leave me tonight! Let us speak till morning of the joys of the heavenly life." He responded, "What are you saying, sister? There is no way I can remain outside the monastery!"
>
> 3. Now the sky was so clear that not a cloud could be seen. When the nun heard her brother's refusal, she put her hands on the table with the fingers intertwined. Then she put her

---

[18] See *Dial.* II.XXXIII.1-5 (123–25).

head on her hands to pray to almighty God. When she raised her head from the table, there was such thunder and lightning and such a downpour of rain that neither venerable Benedict nor the brothers who were with him could set foot outdoors. The nun, by bowing her head in her hands, flooded the table with tears and in this way changed a clear sky into rain. The rain did not follow long after her prayers, but the coincidence of the prayer and the downpour was such that the thunder roared when she raised her head. And the rain fell as soon as she raised her head.

4. When the man of God saw that he could not return to the monastery because of the thunder and lightning and because of the cloudburst, he was dismayed and said, "God forgive you sister. What have you done?" She answered, "Look, I asked you and you wouldn't listen. So I asked my Lord, and he listened. Now leave me if you can and go back to the monastery." He could not, however, go outside the shelter. He was not willing to remain freely there, so he had to remain against his will. And so it happened that they stayed up all night, and they satisfied each other with holy discourse on the spiritual life.

5. . . . . instead of what he wanted, he encountered a miracle wrought by almighty God, at the heartfelt prayer of a woman. It is not surprising that the woman who wished to visit longer with her brother was more effective than he was on that occasion. For according to the sayings of John, ". . . God is love" (1 John 4:8). So it was entirely right that she who loved more should accomplish more.

In this episode, Gregory's story extols Scholastica's superior growth in love, in the face of Benedict's rigid adherence to law. Through Scholastica's prayerful appeal to God, Benedict is humbled and forced to spend the entire evening outside the monastery, which is patently against the monastery's rule. Here they participate in holy conversation and praise of God together to their mutual benefit. It seems obvious that Scholastica is used by Gregory as a *trope*, an example as it were, to make the point that the journey to saintliness is not dependent on law but on love. Adalbert de Vogüé concludes that this story recalls that of Luke's account of the Pharisee and the sinner. Here Scholastica is positioned as the sinner who loves more and, shockingly, Benedict becomes the Pharisee. Yet he shifts this scandalous position of the male saint by recalling the woman who washes the feet of Jesus and Mary of Bethany:

> In order not to remain on the rather unpleasant parallel, let us note that our saint is also identified with Christ, in that he is the object of his sister's love. Just as the sinner loves Jesus, so Scholastica loves Benedict. It is Benedict who plays the role of the beloved Master, whose words are listened to avidly and at length, in a spiritual conversation of which his sister cannot have enough.[19]

Ultimately, for Vogüé, Scholastica remains on the periphery of holiness beside her brother even though she is acclaimed for her "greater love." Significantly, we should note that Gregory also tells us that their conversation was to their "mutual benefit," in contrast to what Vogüé implies above concerning Scholastica's subordination to Benedict's superior wisdom.

The other significant incident in the second *Dialogue* involves Benedict's vision of Scholastica's death soon after this meeting. Here we are told that Benedict sees his sister's soul penetrating heaven in the form of a dove.[20] Scholastica precedes her brother into the heavenly realm and her holi-

---

[19] Vogüé, Gregory the Great, *Life of Saint Benedict*, 161–62. See also Luke 7:36-47 and Luke 10:38-42.

[20] *Dial.* II.XXXIV.1-2 (125).

ness is confirmed. Nevertheless, this is a mere prelude to Benedict's own vision of heaven and glorious death.[21] We hear no more of Scholastica's holiness or how it was that she achieved such progress in the spiritual life. Indeed, history records little more of her, and what we do have comes to us from legends in later medieval lives, homilies, and poems.[22]

If Scholastica is merely a literary invention or *trope* inserted by Gregory, as some scholars would have us believe, then she has nothing more to contribute to our understanding of the significance of women in monastic history, or church history for that matter, nor can she be used as a model to which the contemporary Christian world could aspire. As Boo and Braun note, in this case Scholastica simply remains "chiefly as a character in the life of her illustrious brother . . . hidden in Benedict's shadow."[23] Yet given the early esteem accorded to Scholastica, can we simply be satisfied with this conclusion?[24] Surely there are important questions that remain to be answered if we are to truly appreciate the strength of this woman's love and her significance down through the ages. Without doubt, the question

[21] See *Dial.* II.XXXV.1-8 (131–33).

[22] See, for example, *The Life of St Scholastica* by Alberic of Cassino, eleventh century, in Dom Anselmo Lentini, "L'omilia e la vita di S. Scolastica di Alberic Cassinese," *Benedictina* 3 (1949): 217–38.

[23] Boo and Braun, "Emerging from the Shadows: St. Scholastica," 1.

[24] Scholastica was included in the liturgical calendar by the eighth century, and a church was named after her as early as the eighth century; see Germain Morin, "Les quatre anciens calendriers du Mont-Cassin (VIIIe et IXe siècles)," *Revue Bénédictine* 25 (1908). See also Paul Meyvaert, "The Historical Setting and Significance of the *Codex Benedictus*," *Codex Benedictus (Vat. Lat. 1202), An Eleventh Century Lectionary from Monte Cassino* (New York and Zurich: Johnson Reprint Corporation, 1981, 1982). From Meyvaert's work is it clear that there were lessons for the Night Office on the feast of St. Scholastica used at least as early as the latter part of the ninth century.

of how Scholastica arrived at this superior spiritual position needs investigation, or it might at least legitimately open a door to some imaginative conversation.[25] What was the path of her spiritual development? How did she leave her home in Nursia where, we are told, she was dedicated to God, and later, how did she find a place near her brother in Monte Cassino? How did Scholastica come to have her "own" cell nearby? Was she there before or after Benedict and his monks arrived? Was this "cell" anchoritic, or was she part of a women's religious community—a monastic community? Was she this community's abbess? What was the nature of these annual meetings between Scholastica and Benedict? How do we account for her role as a spiritual mother of a community? What of this final spiritual conversation between the holy siblings? Can we uncover something of the content of this mystical and miraculous encounter? If these conversations were to mutual benefit, what, if anything, was the influence of Scholastica on Benedict, particularly in terms of the Rule he wrote for monks, a Rule we know to be permeated with not just wisdom and discretion, as Gregory tells us in the *Dialogue*, but with love as its driving force?[26] Given that the tradition associates Scholastica's

[25] Boo and Braun have suggested this sort of speculation also. See "Emerging from the Shadows: St. Scholastica," 3.

[26] Note, this emphasis is evident throughout the Rule of Benedict, and particularly so in RB 72, the culmination of the Rule's precepts: "Just as there is an evil and bitter zeal that separates one from God and leads to hell, so too there is a good zeal that separates one from evil and leads to God and eternal life. Thus monks should practice this zeal with the warmest love: 'Let them strive to be the first to honor one another' [Rom 12:10]. They should bear each other's weaknesses of both body and character with the utmost patience. They must compete with one another in obedience. No one should pursue what he judges advantageous to himself, but rather what benefits others. They must show selfless love to the brothers. Let them fear God out of love. They should love their abbot

name with Benedictine monasticism, what was the nature of the community she belonged to? Many such questions emerge as we ponder the significance of Scholastica in order to move our gaze towards her and shift her from the margins of monastic history and spirituality to the center of our concern.

Let us imagine for a moment that Gregory actually wrote another *Dialogue* which has been lost to us through the vagaries of time.[27] And let us suppose that this work, now found, continues Gregory's *Dialogue* of Book II and presents a fuller hagiographical life of St. Scholastica that gives her attention equivalent to that afforded her more illustrious brother. Indeed, let us imagine that, in this newly found *Dialogue*, we can find a Scholastica with a spiritual standing quite apart from her famous and holy brother, and one that retrieves the credibility of Scholastica in the place of monastic history in particular, and church history in general.

I have to admit that the attempt at this fictional recovery of a woman's voice is not a totally novel idea. A few examples of this genre include Jostein Gaarder's *Vita Brevis: A Letter to St Augustine*, which purports to be a lost letter from Floria, Augustine's longtime and unnamed mistress.

---

with sincere and humble charity. Let them prefer absolutely nothing to Christ, and may he lead us all together to everlasting life." All English translations of the Rule of Benedict are taken from Terrence G. Kardong, *Benedict's Rule: A Translation and Commentary* (Collegeville, MN: Liturgical Press, 2021), unless otherwise stated.

[27] Tim Vivian asserts, "Something like ninety percent of Classical and Roman literature is lost to us. This realization becomes acute, even heartbreaking, when we think of how very little of the little we have is by women." Tim Vivian, "Courageous Women: Three Desert Ammas—Theodora, Sarah, and Syncletica; A New Translation from the Greek Alphabetical Apophthegmata Patrum, with Introduction, Notes, and Comments," *American Benedictine Review* 71, no. 1 (2020): 75.

Here, Gaarder presents an inventive and playful re-reading of Augustine's life through the eyes of the woman he loved, and accords her philosophical prominence.[28] Jill Dalladay's *The Abbess of Whitby: A Novel of Hild of Northumbria* attempts to present a credible, if fictitious, story of Hild's background, filling in the lacunae of history in the genre of a novel.[29] And, more recently, Paula Gooder's two studies of Phoebe and Lydia draw on what she claims as "creative historical imagination" to convey Pauline theology through the recovered lives of two important biblical women.[30]

However, I do not know of any attempt as yet to retrieve the life of a woman saint from the past through the use of the ancient hagiographical method. Why bother, you might ask? What is the point if none of this is factual?[31] Yet here is precisely where the recovery of the hagiographical method, used as a "disciplined imagination,"[32] and particularly with its concentration on truth rather than mere fact, can be a tool in the repositioning of women's lives in history.

[28] Jostein Gaarder, *Vita Brevis: A Letter to St Augustine*, trans. Anne Born (London: Phoenix, 1997).

[29] Jill Dalladay, *The Abbess of Whitby: A Novel of Hild of Northumbria* (Oxford: Lion Fiction, 2015).

[30] Paula Gooder, *Phoebe: A Story* (London: Hodder & Stoughton, 2018); and *Lydia: A Story* (London: Hodder & Stoughton, 2022).

[31] Bruno Krusch (d. 1940), with his application of scientific objectivity in his work for *Monumenta Germaniae Historica* (MGH), was not much impressed by hagiography himself, claiming that it was *kirchliche Schwindelliteratur*, "bogus ecclesiastical literature." See Palmer, *Early Medieval Hagiography*, 70. The phrase originally appeared in Bruno Krusch, "Zur Florians- und Lupus-Legende: Eine Entgegnung (Fortsetzung)," *Archiv der Gesellschaft für ältere deutsche Geschichtskunde* 24 (1899): 533–70 (559).

[32] I am grateful to Chris Monaghan, CP, for the suggestion of this terminology, which he learned from one of his students in biblical studies at Yarra Theological Union, a member College of the University of Divinity, Melbourne, Victoria.

From shadowy figures in the life of male holiness, women can be reconfigured as central figures who speak not only to the development of holiness within the Church, but also as examples of how women of history can continue to be powerful and inspiring models of this holiness in their own right for the life of the Church today. In this sense, hagiography becomes a tool which does not pretend to present factual history. However, it does have a legitimate claim to credibly express the truth surrounding the holiness of women whose lives have been of little value in the life of the Church, except for the position they take beside their more formally recognized male counterparts.

By presenting a "lost life" of St. Scholastica as a plausible inclusion in the hagiographical record through this "disciplined imagination," I am attempting to use the same symbolic world view, contextualization, structural composition, and literary techniques as were employed by Gregory himself and other hagiographers of the past.

These writers were not motivated simply by historical fact, but were more focused on biblical examples to help shape the truth of their narratives. Scriptural allusions were therefore the driving force in this ancient hagiographical genre. If the subject of the story did not embody the words and works of Christ or other biblical models and memories, then there was no real basis for their holiness or status as a saint. Thus, for Scholastica's life to convey her holiness, these biblical references must continue to take center stage in my creation of her life story. Therefore, I too have chosen to put the life of Scholastica in a distinctly biblical key, with the Scriptures continually permeating the story. Sometimes this inclusion occurs through direct allusion, as is the case with the story of the wounded Goth where Luke's Good Samaritan parable is likely to be patently obvious to the reader. Likewise, in Scholastica's miraculous calming of a storm, the biblical narrative is obvious and Mark's Gospel parallel needs no emphasizing. In other sections of the story the scriptural allusions may appear to be more subtle, as in the case of the birth of Scholastica and Benedict, where Old Testament models come to the fore.

It is fair to say that ancient hagiographical works are unapologetic about the degree of license they take in terms of literary invention and moral imperative. They risk this approach in order to emphasize a profound truth about their subjects. I have also afforded myself this luxury at times. This is particularly clear in relation to Scholastica's birth, her education, her journey on the dangerous roads from Nursia through southern and central Italy, and her formation of a community in Cassino.[33] As Grant Wacker suggests, the purpose here is not to create "*the* credible story," but rather, "*a* credible story" by embracing "the elasticity of the evidence."[34]

The political and ecclesiastical agendas of hagiographers also found a fertile home within this ancient literature. A primary example of this technique can be found in Athanasius's best-selling *Vita Antonii*, the Life of Antony.[35] Here the bishop presents not only a life of Antony for edification and emulation, but also infuses it with his own christological concerns and arguments against his opponents, groups he considered heretical in his context such

---

[33] For example, the anatomical impossibility of Scholastica's birth is obviously problematic. The location and formation of Scholastica's community is also clearly an issue, and as scholars have continued to argue about this over the years, I felt free to suspend some of the facts in this regard.

[34] Grant Wacker, "Promises (and Perils) of the 'New Hagiography,' " *Fides et Historia* 49, no. 2 (2017): 46.

[35] See Athanasius, *The Life of Antony and the Letter to Marcellinus*, trans. Robert C. Gregg (New York: Paulist Press, 1980).

as the Arians and Melitians. Gregory, in his *Dialogues*, was himself concerned with demonstrating how Christ was still operative in his own context—a world of "catastrophic change," beset with plague, famine, and wars.[36] Thus, the present narrative admits to treading this well-worn path through the contextual, theological, and educational agendas that surround the recovery of a woman's voice of the past by a woman of the twenty-first century, a Good Samaritan Sister of the Order of St. Benedict, for a twenty-first-century Christian Church.[37] I think these agendas will be easily recognizable to the reader, particularly in terms of the feminine weave with which the story has been sewn together.

It should be apparent to some readers that I have at times deliberately cast Scholastica as a Good Samaritan Sister of the Order of St. Benedict. Here I am knowingly imposing limitations on the telling of this story with my own point of view. I trust the reader's willingness to forgive this partiality. The technique again accords with the hagiographical methodology, where the agenda and even the identity of the author takes control of the fabric of the narrative in order to infuse the story with particular concerns.

The hagiographical genre is a dynamic one. As I have already explained, its primary model was originally biblical, with the life of Christ taking center stage. The identity with Christ was, and still is, the truth of any saint's life. However,

---

[36] For a full account of Gregory's context, see R. A. Markus, *Gregory the Great and His World* (Cambridge: Cambridge University Press, 1997).

[37] As Sara Alpern and others have noted, it is with "heightened consciousness of the role of gender" that women write about women. See Sara Alpern, Joyce Antler, Elisabeth Israels Perry, and Ingrid Winther Scobie, eds., "Introduction," in *The Challenge of Feminist Biography: Writing the Lives of Modern American Women* (Urbana: University of Illinois Press, 1992), 10.

the ancient writers of the lives of saints often drew on models created from previous writers.[38] Indeed, many of the stories in the *Life of Benedict* have precedents in the past. So, for example, Benedict's temptations at the beginning call to mind the violent temptations of Antony the Great.[39] I have assumed this perspective in the creation of Scholastica's life by drawing from models that preceded her, such as *The Life of Macrina* by Gregory of Nyssa. In a similar vein, this *Life of Scholastica*, which purports to be a sixth-century creation, ought to feel as if it is a story that is drawn on by later hagiographical lives. In order to achieve this character, I have used later lives, such as *The Life of St. Radegunde* and *The Life of Saint Leoba*, to shape some of the events in the narrative. The aim here is to create the illusion of Scholastica's life as the model for later writers.

Perhaps the most significant change to this style which I have made, so that the story can be sensed as more palatable to the twenty-first-century context, is to downplay any overconcentration on miracles, and to stress the ministerial and missionary role that Scholastica plays in her dealings with her own family, her community, and the world around her. In this sense, I have attempted to dramatically "resist the domestication of female authority" as is so often typical of hagiographers.[40] In the *Life of Benedict* Gregory often

[38] Vogüé draws our attention to this aspect of the monastic tradition in particular, which he claims "began in the West with the seminal *Life of St. Martin* by Sulpicius Severus and also his Letters and Dialogues." See Vogüé, Gregory the Great, *Life of Saint Benedict*, vi.

[39] Vogüé pinpoints many of these sorts of corresponding stories in earlier hagiographical texts throughout his commentary on the *Life of Benedict*.

[40] See Marie Anne Mayeski, "Baudonivia's Life of St. Radegunde: A Theology of Power," in *Women at the Table: Three Medieval Theologians* (Collegeville, MN: Liturgical Press, 2004), 105–47.

breaks into periods of moral or theological teaching for his dialogue partner, Peter the Deacon. I have chosen to follow his lead in this performance. The reader will find that I sometimes paraphrase Gregory's own theological ideas and sometimes quote him directly, either briefly or at length, depending on what I deem necessary in order to make Gregory's teaching distinctive. At other times I have again taken a degree of license with Gregory's thought, so as to put my own theological positions and objections to the forefront. It may seem strange to the reader to see such modern arguments for the equality of women in the spiritual journey placed on the lips of the famous sixth-century pope. However, once more, this is a legitimate technique of hagiographers, who often claimed the voice of a respected teacher to promote their own concerns in their own time and context.

Benedict is famous for his monastic Rule which is full of wisdom and discretion, as Gregory tells us at the end of his *Dialogue*.[41] It is now broadly agreed that Benedict's primary source for writing this Rule was the more elaborately florid and odiously rigid *Rule of the Master*, a contemporary rule that was probably never used in practice because of its moral complexity and inflexibility, endless sermonizing, shameless suspicions, and overt authoritarianism.[42] Benedict's deletions, alterations, and additions to this older rule reveal something of the character of the man, his growth in understanding the vagaries of the human heart, and his enduring monastic legacy. As he wrote his "little rule for beginners," it is well recognized that Benedict's

---

[41] See *Dial.* II.XXXVI.1 (139).

[42] See *RB 1980: The Rule of St. Benedict in Latin and English with Notes*, ed. Timothy Fry and others (Collegeville, MN: Liturgical Press, 1981), 79.

attitude to rule and authority changed over time as he experienced the realities of living in community and grew in wisdom and understanding of the human condition.[43] And as Boo and Braun claim, "one can only speculate about Scholastica's possible influence on the spirit of the Rule itself,"[44] particularly given the conversations that are reported between them in Gregory's *Dialogue*. Indeed, I found myself pondering the nature of Benedict and Scholastica's conversations and how her acquired wisdom might have had a direct influence on his writing of the Rule. In this respect, what might we encounter in this "newly discovered" *Dialogue* of St. Gregory the Great? Perhaps we might find the life of a woman whose understanding of the primacy of love was *always* central to her understanding of the spiritual life, and highly influential in the development of the monasticism that Benedict conceived. It will be clearly apparent that I have taken advantage of this perspective in creating Scholastica's life. Just as the scriptural text plays a central role in the story, so too the reader will notice the centrality of the Rule of Benedict. I have often placed the wisdom of the Rule on Scholastica's lips, making her the originator of this penetrating and discerning insight. I have even dared to suggest that many of the Rule's core values, such as obedience, humility, discretion, hospitality, community, and prayer find their basis in her own growth in wisdom and her conversations with Benedict. As such, this does not in any way dispute the role Gregory has given to Scholastica in his *Dialogue*; indeed, it confirms both her close relationship with her brother and her superior understanding of Christian love. However, it does attempt to

---

[43] See Terrence G. Kardong, *Benedict Backwards: Reading the Rule in the Twenty-First Century* (Collegeville, MN: Liturgical Press, 2017).

[44] Boo and Braun, "Emerging from the Shadows: St. Scholastica," 3.

move Scholastica from the margins of the historical record to center stage, with all the relevance and inspiration that the tradition surrounding her implies. Some may find this suggestion fanciful and even a bit forced, yet one will find little in the record to contradict this suggestion.

What I hope I have done here is to create what Boo and Braun desired by extending Gregory's thunderstorm vignette into "a much longer, more serious drama in which Scholastica figures as a woman aware of her own freedom in God."[45] My task here was not to stray too far from the bounds of credibility but to, as Gooder insists, "listen for the whispers within the voices that often do not speak very loudly in our history, the voices of women."[46] Using a "disciplined imagination," rather than simply making it all up, I pray that I have inserted a story of a beloved saint into the hagiographic record of Christianity that will not only delight and inspire readers, but cause them to ponder more searchingly the sources of the wisdom contained in Benedict's remarkable Rule, a Rule that has stood the test of the ages for both women and men across time and place; a Rule that has helped form an understanding of the Christian life that is humane, life-giving, and Christ-like. I also hope that it will present a challenge for the reader to reconsider all those women whose voices have been erased, devalued, or ignored over the centuries, and inspire a "listening carefully" to the whispered words and wisdom of women as we make our journey together into a future full of hope, with Christ and his gospel for our guide.

---

[45] Boo and Braun, 3.

[46] See Paula Gooder, "Phoebe: A Talk by Paula Gooder," recorded live at St Ann with Emmauel Church, Nottingham, September 22, 2019, https://www.youtube.com/watch?v=tsBrJLjb_xQ&t=2951s, accessed May 2023.

The "Lost" Dialogue of Gregory the Great

~

The Life of St. Scholastica

Prologue

PETER: This story you related to me just yesterday concerning the man of God, Benedict, is indeed, most edifying. It is useful for praising God and inspiring one to live a holy and wholesome life. I was grateful to you for sharing this great wisdom with me. Nevertheless, as I lay on my bed last night, I found that I was driven to a profound curiosity in my thoughts and in my prayers. I would like to know more of what this blessed man and his beloved sister, Scholastica, spoke of on their last meeting, as in this holy conversation there seemed to be such an overwhelming desire for God in both of them. I dare to ask you now about the nature and content of this holy converse of which you spoke.

GREGORY: Your curiosity stems from a hidden desire to deepen your own spiritual journey, Peter, and this is truly a good and wholesome thing. However, it is not possible to answer your question so directly, as it would be beyond your understanding without first telling you a little of this holy woman's story and the great desire for God that she had from the beginning of her life. For you must understand that we do not travel the road to holiness by ourselves. And even Blessed Benedict himself, holy as he was, needed the deep wisdom of his sister for his long and difficult spiritual journey. It is important to realize, Peter, that we seek God together, and sometimes our companions come from unexpected crossroads in our lives. In our case, it was a woman who called forth God's miraculous acts from Benedict's compassion;[1] it was women who brought him to the fear of God;[2] it was women who elicited the forgiveness of God through his prayers;[3] and it was finally a woman who showed him the path of love.[4]

You must remember, Peter, that women are not of lesser value in the eyes of God, though it is often that we can, to our own detriment, cast them in the role of temptress, believing them to have inherited the sin of Eve. For your own humility's sake, do not forget that it was clearly both Adam and Eve who sinned against God, and so woman does not hold the sole responsibility for the failings of humankind. Indeed, if we believe that men are superior to women—God forbid—then surely Adam's sin is far more grievous than that of Eve. Both sexes are equally made in God's image, and both are equally saved through the love of God in Jesus Christ. Know then, Peter, that women hold a profound dignity in God's sight, and often reveal to us the image of God in ways we fail to comprehend or expect. This was the case when Blessed Scholastica's love showed forth God's will through her great love for the holy man Benedict.

PETER: This teaching is sobering for me, and I am truly humbled by your words, but please do not hesitate to tell me this story of the wise and Blessed Scholastica, for her great love as a woman of God does intrigue me. And I so wish to know how she came to be at Monte Cassino, and

[1] *Dial.* II.I.2 (2). In this story, it is the tears of Benedict's nurse which elicit his compassionate and miraculous actions.

[2] See *Dial.* II.II.1 (13) and VIII.4 (42). These two stories present beautiful women who test Benedict's resolve.

[3] See *Dial.* II.XXIII.1ff (91ff.). Here the condemnation of the souls of two unruly nuns is reversed through Benedict's prayers.

[4] See *Dial.* II.XXXIII.1-5 (123–25). The famous "thunderstorm" episode wherein Scholastica's greater love thwarts Benedict's will.

also to understand the great mysteries that this saintly pair held in their hearts and shared on that blessed night before they both departed from this earth.

GREGORY: It is right that this story should not remain concealed, Peter, for the last discourse between these blessed siblings was the culmination of their lives, which were dedicated to the double command to love Christ and their neighbor. To remain silent about the life of the holy virgin, Scholastica, who reached the heights of this purest love for Christ, would be a grave error, for her deep and enduring wisdom can help us along our own path to seeking God, and her desire for community will show us that this journey, as I have said, cannot be achieved alone.

As I explained concerning the life of the man of God, Benedict, I did not know all that there was to tell of him, and what I did know I knew from the witnesses to his life.[5] So it is also with his blessed sister Scholastica. I do not know everything that there surely could be to tell of her deep desire for God, but the little that I can relate I learned from three of her own disciples who had lived with her during her final years in their small community at the foot of Monte Cassino.[6] They had been with Scholastica from the beginning, and knew of her holiness from their own experience of daily living in her presence. These were the holy

---

[5] See *Dial.* II. Prol. Kardong does not include the entire Prologue to *Dialogue II* in his translation. For this reference, see Vogüé, Gregory the Great, *Life of Saint Benedict,* 3

[6] Ildefonso Schuster suggests that there is no evidence for Scholastica establishing a community at Cassino, only a hermitage; however, I have taken license in the telling of the story in this instance, as neither is there any compelling evidence to the contrary. See Ildefonso Schuster, *St. Benedict and His Times*, trans. Gregory J. Roettger (St. Louis: Herder, 1951), 338.

and faithful women Fidelia, Speranza, and Desideria.[7] They were the ones who, with the monks Benedict had sent, returned her body to him for burial on that most holy mountain of Cassino after she had departed in death,[8] and to this day, though now old and weary, they continue in their desire to seek God through the wisdom in which their mistress instructed them. This life of prayer and charity towards others has led them to the same clear vision of God's love for all, a vision which Scholastica beheld in her own life. These three devoted sisters, united through their practice of the three theological virtues from which they earned their names, are now spiritual guides to other communities of holy women who long for God with all their hearts.

[7] It is obvious from the Latin derivations of these names that here I am implying that Scholastica is surrounding herself with faith, hope, and love.

[8] See *Dial.* II.XXXIV.2 (125).

Chapter 1

The Birth of Scholastica and Benedict

I. 1 So let us begin our tale of the holy Scholastica and her great desire for God. Do not be surprised, Peter, when I tell you first of Scholastica's birth, for in this telling you will also hear of Blessed Benedict's birth and the mystery of their relationship, the closeness of which was manifest from the very beginning of their lives.[1]

Before they came to be born, their mother, Abundantia,[2] of blessed memory, had a dream wherein she gave birth to two church bells which rang in praise and harmony with

---

[1] Gregory did not bother to insert anything about Benedict's birth in the second of his *Dialogues*. Though not unheard of, this is unusual in hagiography, which seeks to establish the origins of its subject's holiness as early as possible. I have attempted to correct this omission using the tradition that Benedict and Scholastica were indeed twins.

[2] Later tradition (12th century) gives us the names of Scholastica and Benedict's parents as Abundantia and Euproprius (see Petri Diaconi, *De Viris Illustribus Casinensis Coenobii*, Patrologiae Cursus Completus, Series Latina 173, 1009C, edited by J.-P. Migne [Paris: Garnier, 1895]), both of whom were from the free or upper class (*liberiori genere*) according to Peter the Deacon (1109–1159). The *Dialogues* tells us they were free born (*Dial.* II. Prol. [1]). Abundantia literally means abundant, plentiful, and Euproprius combines the Latin words for good and proper.

inexpressible joy throughout all the world.[3] When she awoke from her dream, she wondered what this could mean, and related it all to her husband. They both pondered the mystery of these things in their hearts, for neither of them could understand what this dream could mean.[4]

When she had come to the end of her time, Abundantia first delivered a baby girl, Scholastica. However, determined even then not to be parted from her brother, nor wishing to leave him alone and unaccompanied, Scholastica emerged from her mother's womb holding firmly onto Benedict's hand. Such was her love and concern for him even as a newborn babe that she could not bear to be parted from him. So, born into life together, these infants, destined for God's purpose, were bonded by the love of each other in their common journey of seeking God.[5]

2. It is with some sadness now that I relate to you, Peter, how it was that in this moment of their birth, Scholastica and Benedict lost not only their mother, but their mother's love. The good and gracious Abundantia gave all that she had of life in order that they might live the plenitude of her own desire for love. She gave up her spirit to the Lord as soon as she had given her children to the world.

3. In naming his children Benedict and Scholastica, their father, Euproprius, prophetically indicated the spirit of godly lives his two children would live, and indeed,

[3] This birth contrasts the prediction given to Rebecca for the birth of Esau and Jacob in Genesis 25:23. Here, rather than conflict, the dream is one of harmony.

[4] See Luke 2:19.

[5] I am playing on the story of the birth of Esau and Jacob from Genesis 25:19-26 here as in above.

Scholastica's love of learning and her desire for God[6] describe the full content of her life as well as the meaning of her name. You will remember, Peter, that we have already heard tell of Benedict's name and its significance in his life.[7]

Even from an early age the spirit of learning was evident in Scholastica's constant questioning of all that surrounded her both in nature and in thought, so much so that her father, who was still grieving the loss of his beloved wife, decided to dedicate his somewhat precocious and inquisitive daughter to God at an early age, in this way hoping to channel her boundless energy towards the pursuit of virtue. As Hannah dedicated Samuel to serve God all the days of his life in the temple, so Euproprius offered Scholastica.[8] Thus it was that she had been taught the Word of the Lord from her infancy by the local priest, and was guided in the way of prayer daily by her own devoted and loving father.

---

[6] Here I draw from the title of Jean Leclercq's seminal work, *The Love of Learning and the Desire for God: A Study of Monastic Culture*, trans. Catharine Misrahi (New York: Fordham University Press, 1982).

[7] See *Dial.* II. Prol. (1), "There was a man of venerable life, who was Blessed (Benedictus), in both grace and name."

[8] See 1 Sam 1. In the *Dialogues*, Gregory has Scholastica dedicated to God as a child. See *Dial.* II.XXXIII.2 (123).

Chapter 2

Scholastica and Sophia

II. 1 In time Euproprius, a man of prudence and good judgment, saw fit to continue the education of both his children in the way of wisdom and fear of the Lord, and they both continued to grow in the love and knowledge of God.[1] The holy man of God, Benedict, we have already heard spoken about at length. Now when it came time for Benedict to leave for his own studies in Rome, Scholastica, anxious and deeply saddened, was found in constant prayer. She argued with her brother and tried to convince him and her father, to no avail, that this decision would only lead him into the temptations of the city and make him full of vainglory and pride.[2]

When he finally left, she was inconsolable, and more so because her fervent prayer and tears had seemed un-

[1] See "The fear of the Lord is the beginning of wisdom" (Prov 9:10). The fear of the Lord is integral to the first step of humility in the Rule of Benedict: "The first step of humility is to utterly flee forgetfulness by keeping the fear of God always before one's eyes" (RB 7.10).

[2] See Macrina's concern for her younger brother, Basil, on his return from his studies in Constantinople. Gregory of Nyssa, *The Life of Macrina*, 8:1-3, in *Macrina the Younger, Philosopher of God*, Medieval Women–Texts and Contexts, trans. Anna M. Silvas (Turnhout, Belgium: Brepols, 2008), 117.

answered. It appeared to her that the bond of love they shared was to be broken, and she struggled within herself to reconcile her desire to understand God's will and her own need for Benedict's presence in her life. Indeed, once Benedict was gone, she wrote constantly to him, urging him to return to their tranquil home.

2. Yet, in a short time, Scholastica's prayer was indeed answered, but not in the way that she had then desired, for her love was not yet purified by the discipline of discernment, the mother of all virtues.[3] You see, Peter, Euproprius cared greatly not only for his son's education but for his daughter's also, and seeing her distress at Benedict's departure, he employed a Greek nurse, Sophia by name, who was of considerable learning herself, so that there would be someone of wise bearing to accompany Scholastica in her studies.[4] In this way, Euproprius hoped to distract her through her deep love of learning.

Sophia was exacting and firm as well as wise and gentle, and before long became Scholastica's spiritual mother and mentor as well as teacher. A Christian by birth, she dedicated herself to Scholastica's upbringing, further encouraging not only her thirst for knowledge but also a deep and abiding love for the Word of God. Sophia continued and deepened Scholastica's study of the Scriptures. Here she found a mirror wherein to see and understand her relationship with

[3] See John Cassian, *Conf.* 2.II.4 (42–43) and RB 64.19. All citations from John Cassian are taken from *John Cassian: The Conferences*, trans. Boniface Ramsey, Ancient Christian Writers, No. 57 (New York: Newman Press, 1997).

[4] "Sophia," the Greek word for wisdom, places Scholastica's teacher firmly within a scriptural warrant of "fear of the Lord." In giving Scholastica a teacher from Greece, I am able to give her access to the Greek hagiographical stories that would otherwise be unavailable to her at this time.

God.[5] Of all the Scriptures, she particularly loved studying the Wisdom of Solomon and singing the psalms. Throughout the day, wherever she was, these psalms were her constant companion.[6] Indeed, Sophia made the psalter Scholastica's textbook, and nature, with all its godly joy, her playground.

Without quashing a young girl's obvious enthusiasm for life, Sophia taught Scholastica the unspeakable joy of God's mysteries. Experienced in the practice of deep silence and stillness, she reminded Scholastica of the pervasive presence of God in—and the love of Christ for—all persons and all things. As models, Sophia read Scholastica the wondrous stories of Blessed Thecla, and these caused her great delight as she imagined herself a co-worker with Paul and bravely persevering in her faith to the end.[7] However, it was in the stories from the life of the most holy and sainted Macrina, which Sophia also brought with her from her home country, that Scholastica gained both her love of wisdom sought in silent contemplation and the practice of charity in the marketplace. Indeed, Sophia gave to Scholastica this secret

[5] See Jas 1:23-24.

[6] An allusion to *Life of Macrina*, 4:3-4 (113–14). "Instead the parts of the God-inspired Scripture that seem more easily learned at a young age: these formed the child's lessons, especially the Wisdom of Solomon, and besides this, whatever bears on the moral life. Indeed, there was nothing whatever of the Psalter that she did not know, since she recited each part of the psalmody at its own proper time. When she rose from bed, or began her duties or rested from them, or sat down to eat or retired from table, when she went to bed or rose from it for prayers, she kept up the psalmody wherever she went, like a good travelling companion that never left her at any time." See Anna Silvas's introduction for a sketch of further details of Blessed Macrina's life.

[7] See *The Acts of Paul and Thecla*, trans. Jeremiah Jones (Kerry, Ireland: CrossReach Publications, 2019).

name—Macrina—because of her hunger for virtue and her pursuit of philosophy.[8]

3. PETER: I am astounded at the wisdom of these women and how God saw fit to bestow his gifts upon them.

GREGORY: You may wonder at this pursuit of philosophy and the gift of wisdom in a woman, Peter. Yet why is it that we would consider these things impossible at worst, and improbable at best? How is it that wisdom resides in a woman, you say? It is pride alone, Peter, that leads us to question such a thing. Wisdom, Peter, is a gift of the Holy Spirit, who, like "the wind blows where it chooses, and you hear the sound of it, but you do not know where it comes from or where it goes."[9] Indeed, the Apostle indicates this when considering our own call to follow the Lord: "not many of you were wise by human standards, not many were powerful, not many were of noble birth. But God chose what is foolish in the world to shame the wise; God chose what is weak in the world to shame the strong; God chose what is low and despised in the world, things that are not, to reduce to nothing things that are, so that no one might boast in the presence of God."[10] Thus we must not be surprised that God bestows wisdom on those whom you may consider the weaker sex. Indeed, Peter, you must not be astounded at all to find that women are often the stronger in the faith, as this story of Benedict and Scholastica has already demonstrated to you.[11]

---

[8] Macrina's secret name was Thecla, *Life of Macrina*, 3:1 (112). Gregory of Nyssa maintains that Macrina's life met the ideal of a life of philosophy, *Life of Macrina*, 7:5 (116). It is important to note that in the ancient world "philosophy" referred to a way of life—a life of seeking wisdom.

[9] John 3:8.

[10] 1 Cor 1:26-29.

[11] See *Dial.* II.XXXIII.5 (124).

4. For what then is wisdom? We are, indeed, all called to this life of philosophy, which is this love of wisdom. Job tells us: "Truly, the fear of the Lord, that is wisdom."[12] And what is this "fear of the Lord" so that we may have wisdom? Is it not to have the remembrance of the presence of God at all times and in all places?[13] This, then, is the fear of the Lord, which itself comes from God, and by which we attain wisdom. To acknowledge the presence of God in all persons is the fear of the Lord, and to know the presence of God in all things is to know the fear of the Lord. Wisdom, then, discerns when to stand in awe of God's presence in silence and listen with the ear of the heart, or when to praise the mystery of God's presence with speech. Wisdom also discerns when to act in bringing God's love to our neighbor and our world. Indeed, "To fear the Lord is the root of wisdom, and her branches are long life."[14]

There is so much more I want to say to you about wisdom, Peter, but let us return to our subject, Blessed Scholastica, in whom this wisdom began to grow into its full flowering.

5. Scholastica held Sophia in high esteem and lovingly learned to serve and obey her in all humility, although it was Sophia who was her maid and teacher. In this respect, Sophia taught Scholastica the meaning of humility by her own deeds. At all times and in all places, Sophia considered all her thoughts and actions to be under the loving and watchful eye of God, and she taught Scholastica never to forget this truth.[15] Indeed, there was also a fruitful exchange between them, which grew to be not just a relationship of

12 Job 28:28.
13 See RB 7—the first step of humility.
14 Sir 1:20.
15 See RB 7.14.

respect but also one of loving mutuality. And this was so, despite the fact that one was the older and wiser, and the other the younger and guileless. In this way, Scholastica's prayer was answered, for although she lost the presence of her brother, she gained a deep and abiding hunger for the same wisdom that he also sought. And thus she slowly grew to maturity and was fired by the love of Christ and increased in her desire for wisdom and its fruits. She fixed her heart always on reading and hearing the Word of God, and she committed all this not simply to her memory, but also to putting it into practice whenever the opportunity arose, and in this way she fulfilled the command to "pray without ceasing."[16] Not only was she at prayer in her own private room, but also in the inner chamber of her heart, whether she was sitting or walking, working with her hands or even lying down to sleep.

6. Scholastica obeyed her father and Sophia in all things and tried to imitate the good qualities of each, modeling herself on the wisdom and cheerfulness of one and the virtue and patience of the other.[17] And before all else she practiced the love of Christ in her actions, for without this she knew that any other virtue was void.

7. In all this time, holy Scholastica continued to write to her blessed brother Benedict while he was away at school in Rome. In these letters she would urge him to remain steadfast in his love of God and neighbor and to prefer nothing to the love of Christ.[18] She reminded him that God sees all our thoughts and actions, and exhorted him to listen

[16] 1 Thess 5:17.

[17] See Antony of Egypt, who learned the virtues from the elders with whom he associated. See *Vita Antonii*, 3 in, Athanasius, *Life of Antony and the Letter to Marcellinus*, 32.

[18] See RB 4.21.

intently to holy reading and to give himself frequently to prayer.[19] He, in his turn, tried to console her with his own letters of reply, and assured her of his desire for virtue and his faithful love of God, though he did express his distress at the licentious style of life of the other students who surrounded him day and night in Rome.[20] Nevertheless, in spite of this exchange and Benedict's reassurance, Scholastica did not believe that Benedict was listening intently to her when she would extol to him the benefits of a life dedicated to God. Sophia tried insistently to bring Scholastica to understand the humble importance of trusting in God's providential care of Benedict and not her own desire to have him with her. She further instructed her through prayer and good works to turn the memory of her brother towards a deeper memory of Christ in her daily tasks and the readings that were assigned to her. Through this instruction, Sophia impressed upon Scholastica the need to never lose hope in God or God's mercy.[21]

8. PETER: Sophia is indeed true to her name when she exhorts Scholastica to trust in God's mercy.

GREGORY: Indeed, Peter, you have correctly understood the deeper meaning of Sophia's name. For wisdom finds its home in trust in the Lord's mercy and not in one's own insights or efforts.[22] For what is mercy but the hand of God lifting us to his presence in time of need? As the Psalmist tells us: "How precious is your steadfast love, O God! / All people may take refuge in the shadow of your wings. / They feast on the abundance of your house, / and you give them drink from the river of your delights. / For

[19] See RB 4.1-2, 48, and 55-56.
[20] *Dial.* II. Prol. (Vogüé, 3).
[21] See RB 4.41 and 74.
[22] See Prov 3:5.

with you is the fountain of life; / in your light we see light."[23] Without the mercy of God, we would never know God's light, for it is impossible for us to achieve virtue on our own merits. Indeed, in all things we are totally dependent on the mercy of God, in both our good habits, which are brought about only through God's ever-present grace, and in our bad habits, when we are in need of God's generous forgiveness.

Thus it was that being schooled in the Scriptures herself, Sophia was leading Scholastica towards a quietness of mind in relation to her anxiety for her brother, and a humility patterned on that of Christ as well as a dependency on God's mercy. All this training was leading her to a love far greater than she could have imagined in any earthly desire, even her constant desire for her beloved brother, Benedict.[24]

---

[23] Ps 36:7-9.

[24] See RB 7.31-33—the second step of humility: "The second step of humility is not to delight in satisfying our desires out of love for our own way. Rather, we should pattern our behavior on that saying of the Lord: *I have not come to do my own will but the will of him who sent me* [John 6:38]. Scripture also says: *Self-will brings punishment [on itself] but obedience to duty merits a reward.*"

Chapter 3

The First Dream of Scholastica and the Prophecy of Sophia

III. 1 During these early years, Scholastica remained living in her father's house in Nursia, with her nurse and teacher Sophia. Fixing her gaze on heavenly things through discipline of thought and the practice of virtue, she grew, as I have said, in love and knowledge of God.[1] At one time she had a dream which greatly perplexed her. In the dream she beheld a lump in her heart and drew from it a beautiful golden bell which she cast above her and gazed at for some time in wonder and awe. Soon she began to ring the bell, and its sound was so sweet that she rang it to anyone who would care to listen. From out of the bell poured forth many smaller bells which rang in harmony around it, and all who heard these bells were drawn to listen intently to the sweetness of their harmonious and impelling music. When she woke from her sleep, she wondered what this dream could mean, but being both hesitant to reveal the joy that she had experienced in the dream and anxious to know its meaning, she told no one of it.

---

[1] Allusion to the growth of Jesus in wisdom and years, Luke 2:52.

2. Sophia, who in her experience of life and wisdom was able to read the hearts of many, became increasingly aware that Scholastica was hiding some secret thought from her.[2] And so it was that on one day, when they were alone together reading from Scripture and discussing its deeper meaning, Sophia read the words of St. Paul:

> For it is not the hearers of the law who are righteous in God's sight, but the doers of the law who will be justified. When Gentiles, who do not possess the law, do instinctively what the law requires, these, though not having the law, are a law to themselves. They show that what the law requires is written on their hearts, to which their own conscience also bears witness; and their conflicting thoughts will accuse or perhaps excuse them on the day when, according to my gospel, God, through Jesus Christ, will judge the secret thoughts of all.[3]

On hearing these final words of the reading, Scholastica broke into tears, for her thoughts were indeed conflicted. Sophia bent towards her, and gently taking her by the hand, said to her, "What is it you wish to tell me, my child? What are your secret thoughts that need to be revealed?"[4] Scholastica then unburdened herself of her dream to Sophia, and Sophia prayed for discernment in stillness and silence. When some time had passed, she said to Scholastica, "Has

[2] See Rudolf, Monk of Fulda, *The Life of Saint Leoba*, in *The Anglo-Saxon Missionaries in Germany: Being the Lives of SS. Willibrord, Boniface, Sturm, Leoba, and Lebuin, Together with the Hodoeporicon of St. Willibald and a Selection from the Correspondence of St. Boniface*, trans. Charles H. Talbot (New York: Sheed and Ward, 1954), 221.

[3] Rom 2:13-16.

[4] The revelation of thoughts to an elder by a disciple is a rich tradition within monasticism, reaching back to the Desert Mothers and Fathers. It is a tradition that the Rule of Benedict also picks up, e.g., RB 4.50.

your father not told you of the dream your mother had before you were born?" "No, he has not," replied Scholastica. And Sophia then related the contents of her mother's dream to her.

"Let me now tell you the meaning of this dream of yours," said Sophia. "The bell you saw in your dream is the love of God that he has set within you. The motion of the bell you see swings earthward through works of mercy in love of neighbor, and swings heavenward through contemplation of the love of God. Hence its harmonious and sweet sound. Indeed, God has called you and your brother to ring his love throughout all the land and confer benefits on many people, but before you can undertake this great mission from God, you must first learn what it means to love God and your neighbor through humility and charity." In this way, Scholastica was led through Sophia's wise and insightful counsel to deepen her understanding of God's call for her.

3. PETER: I am again amazed at the insightful wisdom of this foreigner, Sophia. Tell me of this gift of reading hearts which she clearly possessed in her guidance of holy Scholastica.

GREGORY: You are right, Peter, to say that Sophia had a gift for reading hearts. In our desire for God, we often find that our "heart is distracted with diversity of things, and as our minds are divided among many interests, they become confused."[5] Indeed, we become "delinquent of heart as the heart deserts us whenever it slips away through evil thoughts,"[6] through a lack of attention on the Word of God

[5] See *Gregory the Great, Regulae Pastoralis* 1:4, in Gregory the Great, *Pastoral Care (Regulae Pastoralis)*, trans. Henry Davis, Ancient Christian Writers, No. 11 (New York: Newman Press, 1950/1978), 27.

[6] See *Pastoral Care* 3:14 (130).

in our lives. Sophia herself had long struggled with her own thoughts and desires, and through her daily reading of the Scriptures, deep reliance on prayer, and the wise counsel of others, was able to achieve what the ancients call single-ness of heart.[7] Sophia had acquired that miracle of discern-ment through the Spirit whereby one is able to be a physician of souls.[8] By always bringing Scholastica deeper and deeper into the presence of the Word of God, Sophia was able to teach Scholastica how to confront her own thoughts, and her wise insights helped her safely navigate them, discerning which were from God and which were from the evil one.

4. PETER: This discernment of thoughts in order to read hearts must be a gift of the Spirit, surely?

GREGORY: This is truly so, Peter. For as the Apostle proclaims, "To one is given through the Spirit the utterance of wisdom, and to another the utterance of knowledge ac-cording to the same Spirit, to another faith by the same Spirit, to another gifts of healing by the one Spirit, to an-other the working of miracles, to another prophecy, to an-other the discernment of spirits."[9] For the Spirit brings into the light that which lies hidden in darkness. And those with this truly heavenly gift can discern their neighbor's thoughts and can gaze transparently into their hearts.[10]

PETER: I am full of wonder concerning this gift, but please continue with this story of these women and their wisdom, for I am captivated by their desire for virtue.

[7] See Cassian, *Conf.* 9.XIV (329ff.).
[8] See *Pastoral Care* 1:1 (21).
[9] 1 Cor 12:8-10.
[10] See *Dial.* IV.43 (250–51).

Chapter 4

Mission to the Village of Nursia

IV. 1 GREGORY: In those early days Scholastica could often be found sitting with her father, Euproprius, listening with a compassionate heart to his struggles as he continued to grieve the loss of his beloved wife, Abundantia. She would gradually dry his tears with talk of God's loving embrace of her mother in his heavenly kingdom. And she would encourage him in his attention to prayer and to a practical love of God by urging him to attend benevolently to the workers in his fields and to the many poor people who resided in their village of Nursia. And so it was that soon Euproprius was daily seen working alongside his servants in both their home and the fields, sharing in their labors as a brother to them, and caring for them in their poverty when need arose. Besides this service, he could often be found praying in the little parish church or distributing alms to the poor of the village. In this way, his grief at losing the love of his blessed wife was gradually turned towards a love for Christ through love of others.

2. One day when Scholastica and her father were celebrating the Lord's Supper at the Sunday gathering in their local church, she heard read the parable of the Good Samaritan from the Gospel of Luke.[1] Taking the words into

[1] See Luke 10:25-37.

her heart, Scholastica felt the call to "go and do likewise" personally addressed to her.[2] From that day on, she would always go with her father to visit the sick and poor of the town. Together with Sophia they would daily sing psalms in the church, and the sound of their mellifluous voices would draw others to join them in praise and thanksgiving for God's abundant gifts to them all.

---

[2] A direct allusion to a similar call experienced by Antony the Great on hearing the Gospel read in his parish church: "And he went into the church pondering these things, and just then it happened that the Gospel was being read, and he heard the Lord saying to the rich man, *If you would be perfect, go, sell what you possess and give to the poor, and you will have treasure in heaven.*" *Vita Antonii* 2 (31), emphasis mine.

Chapter 5

The Miracle of Bread

V. 1 At one time there was a famine in the country, and many came to Nursia seeking shelter and food.[1] Because of the reports that had circulated about her family's extraordinary reputation for goodness of life and charity, many came to Scholastica's home seeking relief and comfort.[2]

Scholastica and Sophia would spend their time baking bread night and day, and Euproprius would distribute it to those in need, both in the town itself and to those who came knocking at his door, desperately searching for food and a kind word. So great were the numbers of the hungry and destitute that it soon seemed that there would be no end to their great demand for care. Euproprius worried about how long their own grain stores could support such need, but Scholastica was eager to see that no one, no matter who they were, went without, and insisted that none should be turned away. Nevertheless, given their dwindling supplies, it came about that both Euproprius and Sophia confronted

---

[1] Recent studies have suggested that the various famines and plagues that rocked Western Europe at the time of the decline of the Roman Empire may have been due to factors connected to climate change. See Kyle Harper, *The Fate of Rome: Climate, Disease, and the End of an Empire* (Princeton: Princeton University Press, 2017).

[2] See *Life of Macrina*, 14:6 (123–24).

Scholastica with rational arguments, pleading with her to stop taking in so many homeless wanderers and strangers, or else they too would be left destitute.[3] Scholastica countered their words with those of Scripture, insisting that in turning away one of these "little ones" they could well be turning away Christ himself, and she exclaimed the words of Truth: "I was a stranger and you welcomed me."[4] "Surely," she urged, "Christ is especially present in these needy and hungry people."[5]

2. God's grace shone through Scholastica's words and actions, for just as in the days of Elijah when the widow's jar of meal was not emptied nor her jug of oil spent,[6] and though Sophia and Scholastica kneaded and baked bread daily, their stores of grain did not diminish nor did their supply of oil fail.[7] There was food for Euproprius to distribute at all times, and there was also never a lack of room for yet another hungry stranger who was always treated as a guest at their table.[8] All were sustained by the bread that they daily broke, blessed, and shared together, until the

[3] Stories about the unbounded generosity of a saint towards the poor can be found in other hagiographical stories, including *The Life of St. Brigit the Virgin by Cogitosus*, in *Celtic Spirituality*, trans. Oliver Davies (New York: Paulist Press, 1999), 124.

[4] Matt 25:35.

[5] See RB 53.7.

[6] See 1 Kgs 17:14.

[7] A similar miracle is recorded in the *Dialogues* during a time of famine. Here it occurs in relation to a distrustful and disobedient monk. See *Dial.* II.XXVIII.2 (102–4). This sort of miracle is also recorded in *The Life of St Radegunde by the Nun, Baudonivia*, in *Handmaids of the Lord: Holy Women in Late Antiquity and the Early Middle Ages*, trans. Joan M. Petersen, Cistercian Studies 143 (Collegeville, MN: Cistercian Publications, 1996), 409.

[8] See RB 53.

drought was broken and the Lord once again sent rain and blessings upon the parched earth.

You can see here, Peter, the great abundance of God's grace that he bestows on those who love him, as Scripture says, "give, and it will be given to you. A good measure, pressed down, shaken together, running over, will be put into your lap; for the measure you give will be the measure you get back."[9] So it is when we share our life with others and we join our lives to Christ, who gave his very self to us.

PETER: This is truly a tale of the virtuous Christian life. Do, I beg you, share more of it with me, your humble servant.

3. GREGORY: Euproprius and Sophia were moved by Scholastica's good zeal and selfless love of others, but most especially by her trust in the providence of God. Indeed, they too joined her in her unstinting generosity. And so it was that their home in Nursia became a refuge for the sick and destitute during this time of crisis. For no one was sent away hungry or without somewhere being made available to shelter them from the cold of the night, the heat of the day, or from any impending harm. Nor were they sent away hungry for spiritual nourishment, as Scholastica would greet each of them with a holy kiss, pray for them when they came to the door, and before they departed she would ask them for a blessing.[10] She would also read to them from the Scriptures and talk of Christ's love for them at all times and in all places.

4. PETER: This quality of living hospitality that we see exhibited by Scholastica and her family is surely a virtue springing from their holy life.

---

[9] Luke 6:38.
[10] See RB 53.5 and 66.3.

GREGORY: Yes, Peter, you have identified this quality precisely. Indeed, we must not pass over this virtuous hospitality too quickly. Let us ponder for a while the story of the Lord's appearance to the disciples on the Road to Emmaus.[11] It is without doubt that the two disciples in this story loved the Lord. However, when he walked beside them they did not recognize his presence. Indeed, they expressed their doubt in him. Yet it was when they offered the Lord hospitality that he revealed to them his identity at the breaking of the bread. Can you understand this, Peter? For it is not by simply hearing the commandments of God that the flame of faith came into their hearts, but rather it was by putting those same commandments into practice through hospitality that their faith burned bright within them. The disciples were able to truly know the Lord when he spoke to them, but only when he allowed them to recognize him through the food that they shared with him. You see, Peter, in this hospitality to a stranger the work of love is performed, and the presence of Christ becomes known. As Paul says, "Do not neglect to show hospitality to strangers, for by doing that some have entertained angels without knowing it."[12] And, as Scholastica pointed out herself, the Truth declares, "I was a stranger, and you welcomed me."[13] We must therefore remember that "the greatest care should be exhibited in the reception of the poor and pilgrims, for Christ is more especially received in them; for the very fear of the rich wins them respect," as you know, and this is not the case with the poor.[14] So, in order to grasp the deeper

---

[11] See Luke 24:13-35. Gregory comments on this passage in his *Homily* 23. See *Forty Gospel Homilies*, trans. David Hurst, Cistercian Studies 123 (Collegeville, MN: Cistercian Publications, 1990), 176–77.

[12] Heb 13:1-2.

[13] Matt 25:35 and *Homily* 23, 177.

[14] RB 53.15.

meaning of this Gospel passage, let us begin by putting into practice what we have already understood.[15]

5. PETER: This is a most profound teaching and one which challenges me in the depths of my soul, particularly given the needs of so many in our own times.[16]

GREGORY: Indeed, Peter. Without this practice of hospitality today, our Christianity would be mere words. As I will further demonstrate in this present story of the holy Scholastica, this "oneness" in Christ Jesus was at the heart of her family's way of life together in Nursia. But let me return now to the many other virtues that you will discover in this holy woman of God, and which are also at the center of our Christian life together.

---

[15] In this section I have summarized and paraphrased much of Gregory the Great, *Homily* 23.

[16] At the time of Gregory the Great's pontificate, the city of Rome had been ravaged by flood, famine, and plague. There were also waves of needy refugees and the constant threat of Lombard invasion. It was also a time of political, social and religious instability. Gregory found himself responsible for much of this multiple complex of circumstances. For a short summary of this context see Hubertus R. Drobner, *The Fathers of the Church: A Comprehensive Introduction* (Peabody, MA: Hendrickson, 2007), 511–15.

Chapter 6

Benedict's Departure from Rome and the Death of Euproprius

VI. 1 As I have indicated, through his own good works and those of his household Euproprius shared his burdens by responding to the needs of others. In this way, he so lightened the weight of his own grief through this selfless service. This way of hospitality converted many to the love of Christ and Christian charity, and some stayed to work and pray on the family property even after the drought was over. Thereby the estate was turned into a community of sorts—making all the sisters and brothers equals with vagabonds, landowners, nurses, the homeless poor, servants, and field workers.[1]

2. Meanwhile, Benedict's letters to his dear sister were of deep concern to Blessed Scholastica, as he continued to write to her concerning the dissipated life of his fellow students and the continuing temptations he faced in the city of Rome. It seemed that her early anxiety had been justified, and her predictions were indeed proving to be a reality. She responded with her ardent prayers and words

---

[1] See *Life of Macrina*, 9 (118). Gregory of Nyssa tells of the social asceticism that Macrina instituted on their family estate.

of deep wisdom. Holy Scholastica urged him to leave Rome and to come home to where he might find the peace of soul that he was looking for, and she exhorted him to keep "the fear of God always before one's eyes."[2] With such words she drew Benedict's thoughts towards a deeper desire for God, and, although Scholastica's wish for her brother to come home was not granted, eventually, as I have already described to you, Peter, in our previous discussion yesterday, he renounced all thought of worldly fame, leaving his studies and the dissolute life of Rome for his cave in Subiaco, in order to find himself in the life of perfection.[3]

3. Soon after this time Euproprius became ill and was gathered into the arms of God—there to meet again his beloved wife, Abundantia, in union with the Trinity and all the saints of heaven. With the holy man of God, Benedict, having given his life to the path of seeking God in solitude and prayer, Blessed Scholastica had now lost both her dearest brother in a manner of death to this life, and her beloved father from this earthly way of life. However, her growth in, and desire for, the spiritual life, along with Sophia's loyal and motherly presence to her, enabled her to rise above the depths of grief and loss she felt within her heart.[4] In this, she became an example of steadfastness, finding within herself the courage to rejoice in all the blessings that God had bestowed on her in spite of her circumstances.[5]

Thus it was that she was left with all her family's land and wealth, and this she continued to administer, with Sophia's wise guidance, towards the pursuit of charity in all things.

[2] RB 7.10—the first step of humility—echoing Ps 36:1.

[3] See *Dial.* II.I.3 (2)

[4] See *Life of Macrina*, 12:1 (120).

[5] See *Life of Macrina*, 12:5 (120–21).

Chapter 7

Scholastica's Way of Life in Nursia

VII. 1 As I have explained to you, Peter, it was in the midst of this service to others that Sophia and Scholastica were eventually joined by other women in their life of prayer and service, some of whom had been left homeless and poor on the wayside because of the drought, and others who were simply drawn to the Christian life that they witnessed in the actions of these holy women. Both Sophia and Scholastica gave instructions more by their deeds than by their words, and whenever they counseled that a particular action was harmful to their spiritual progress, they showed by their own conduct that this action was to be avoided.[1] In this way, they so arranged their life in community that they were loved by all the sisters, and none were in any way afraid of them because of their disciplined and virtuous way of life.[2] Rather, they were encouraged to live charitable and holy lives themselves.

2. Indeed, Scholastica and Sophia followed the path of both Martha and Mary in their manner of life and combined the qualities of both, that is, of outward love and service to their neighbor with interior contemplation of

[1] See RB 2.12-15.
[2] See RB 64.19.

God's love. For one without the other does not fulfill the double command of Christ himself, as when he replied to the lawyer who had asked which was the greatest commandment: "'You shall love the Lord your God with all your heart, and with all your soul, and with all your mind.' This is the greatest and first commandment. And a second is like it: 'You shall love your neighbor as yourself.' On these two commandments hang all the law and the prophets."[3] Giving equal value to both commands, Sophia and Scholastica did well what Martha did so that they could fully hope for what Mary had.[4]

3. PETER: Yet is it not true that the way of Mary is the more desirable? I have heard this said many times.

GREGORY: My dear Peter, anyone who wishes to cling to the sanctuary of contemplation must first discipline themselves in the school of good works. In this way they will come to discern whether they no longer do any harm to their neighbor and whether they can patiently bear wrongs against them from their neighbors. They will also not be overcome by the joy of receiving worldly goods and so cease to perform good works themselves, nor will they be weighed down by excessive sorrow when the goods of this world are withdrawn from them. By this training they will be able to discern whether thoughts of this world's passing things cast a shadow over their desire to withdraw and turn inward to consider spiritual things. And they will know how to prudently prune away these distracting thoughts from their desires for God alone.[5]

[3] Matt 22:37-40.

[4] See Augustine, *Sermon* 104:4, in *The Works of Saint Augustine: A Translation for the 21st Century: Sermons*, Vol. 4, trans. Edmund Hill (Brooklyn, NY: New City Press, 1992), 83.

[5] See Gregory the Great, *Moralia on Job*, Book VI, XXXVII:59, in *Moral Reflections on the Book of Job*, vol. 2: Books 6–10, trans. Brian

What is more, Peter, we can attain the joys of heaven without the contemplative life on condition that good works are not neglected when we are able to do them; so clearly we cannot gain the heavenly life without attention to the active life, particularly should we not do the good we can do even when we are attentive to the contemplative life.[6] They, the active and the contemplative lives, form one way of life which we must strive to achieve.

4. It was through this simple life of charity, detached from material things and directed towards the love of Christ, that holy Scholastica gradually attained a state of profound humility. Indeed, the virtue of humility shone forth from her as the sun shines forth on a green field and brings forth abundant good. Her wealth was in the will of God, and in sharing everything with which she was blessed. Even when this was difficult and tiring, she embraced the struggle with a quiet heart.[7] No work was too lowly or menial for her, and she did not boast of her achievements, but quietly went about her work so as not to draw attention to herself.[8]

5. Scholastica's wisdom grew with each passing day, yet she was neither arrogant nor full of pride even when her words edified her hearers. She did not make distinctions among people but was kind and gracious to everyone, from the lowest beggar to the most noble guest. She was always cheerful and, though of happy countenance, never used laughter to excess or to belittle another.[9] There was never

---

Kerns, Cistercian Studies 257 (Collegeville, MN: Cistercian Publications, 2015), 85–86.

[6] See *Hom. iii in Ezech*, in *Homilies of Saint Gregory the Great on the Book of the Prophet Ezekiel*, trans. Theodosia Gray (Etna, CA: Center for Traditionalist Orthodox Studies, 1990), 35.

[7] See RB 7.35ff.—the fourth step of humility.

[8] See RB 7.49ff.—the sixth step of humility.

[9] See RB 7.59—the tenth step of humility.

a hasty or thoughtless word from her mouth and, should someone test her patience, she never let the sun go down on her anger.[10]

Though lavish in her desire to provide for the material needs of others, she showed moderation in supplying her own basic needs for life. Nevertheless, she displayed great zeal for reading and ceased from it only for the call of regular prayer, to tend to the pressing needs of others, and her body's own sustenance and sleep. Indeed, the Scriptures never left her hands.[11] Knowing that "*the Lord constantly looks down from heaven on the human race to see if there is anyone with the wisdom to seek God*,"[12] she gradually became aware of her own base desires and turned them more and more towards a love of God and her neighbor.

6. In time, Scholastica became renowned for her sacred learning, and was admired for her attention to all the books of the Old and New Testament, which she had learned by heart. To add to this, particularly with Sophia's wise guidance, she read many of the writings of the Church Mothers and Fathers. As I have told you already, Peter, she especially loved the stories of the brave preaching of Thecla, the companion and disciple of Paul,[13] and also the steadfast wisdom of the desert mothers, Sarah and Syncletica.[14] She gasped

[10] See Eph 4:26; RB 4.73; and also *Life of St Radegunde by the Nun, Baudonivia*, 408.

[11] See *Life of St Radegunde by the Nun, Baudonivia*, 408.

[12] See RB 7.27.

[13] See *Acts of Paul and Thecla*. The bibliographical details are given in chapter 2, footnote 7.

[14] See Elizabeth A. Castelli, trans., "Pseudo-Athanasius: The Life and Activity of the Holy and Blessed Teacher Syncletica," in *Ascetic Behavior in Greco-Roman Antiquity: A Sourcebook*, ed. Vincent L. Wimbush (Minneapolis: Fortress Press, 1990); and Benedicta Ward, trans., *The Sayings of the Desert Fathers: The Alphabetical Collection*, Cistercian Studies 59 (Collegeville, MN: Cistercian Publications, 1975).

in wonder at the penitent faith and lives of the prostitutes, Mary of Egypt and Pelagia.[15] She longed to travel to the holy places that Egeria and Melania had visited on pilgrimage.[16] But most assuredly, she aspired to the prayerful and charitable life lived at the heart of the Church by Macrina, whose brothers were the Great Basil and Gregory.[17]

7. The young Scholastica was also moved by Blessed Augustine's teaching on the importance of love over law, and his insistence that "the common good take precedence over the individual" in all her works of charity so that all might live in harmony together.[18] Indeed, she would measure her heart's degree of love by the enlargement of her concern for others. And she was astounded by the Rule of Blessed Basil which Sophia so treasured in all her teachings.[19] It was he who so clearly insisted that it was only in community, rather than alone, that one could fulfill the gospel command to love one another.

8. PETER: But why is this stress on community so marked when you yourself have extolled the lives of so many holy hermits who live in our land?[20]

---

[15] See Benedicta Ward, *Harlots of the Desert: A Study of Repentance in Early Monastic Sources* (Collegeville, MN: Cistercian Publications, 1987).

[16] See *Egeria: Diary of a Pilgrimage*, trans. George E. Gingras, Ancient Christian Writers, No. 38 (New York: Paulist Press, 1970); and Palladius of Aspuna, *The Lausiac History*, trans. John Wortley, Cistercian Studies 252 (Collegeville, MN: Cistercian Publications, 2015), 108–9.

[17] *Life of Macrina*. The bibliographical details are given in chapter 2, footnote 2.

[18] See Augustine, *Praeceptum*, particularly 1 and 5:2, in *Augustine of Hippo and His Monastic Rule*, trans. George Lawless (Oxford: Clarendon, 1987), 81–82, 95.

[19] See *The Rule of St Basil in Latin and English: A Revised Critical Edition*, trans. Anna M. Silvas (Collegeville, MN: Liturgical Press, 2013).

[20] Gregory's first and third *Dialogues* extolls the virtues and lives of the holy men of Italy, many of them hermits.

GREGORY: You are right to ask this question, Peter. However, many of these holy hermits had first undertaken the long hard years of testing in community.[21] Indeed, our blessed Father Basil, in his zeal, saw fit to admonish those who sought to live alone, saying, "Whose feet then will you wash? For whom will you perform the duties of care? In comparison with whom shall you be lower or even the last, if you live by yourself?"[22] It is in the school of community that we make progress in virtue, Peter, for here we learn both obedience and humility, and these virtues perfect our lives in charity.

9. But let me further explain to you, lest you fail to understand the length and breadth and depth of this charity which Christ has shown to us. For Sophia also instilled in Scholastica a profound yearning for the pure, transformative, and mystical prayer of Blessed John Cassian and his teaching on purity of heart. This prayer leads us to a glimpse of eternal life through its power to restore God's image in us for, as John taught us, it comes about that

> every love, every desire, every effort, every undertaking, every thought of ours, everything that we live, that we speak, that we breathe will be God, and when that unity which the Father now has with the Son and which the Son has with the Father will be carried over into our understanding and our mind, so that, just as he loves us with a sincere and pure and indissoluble love, we too may be joined to him with perpetual and inseparable love and so united with him that whatever we breathe, whatever we understand, whatever we speak, may be God.[23]

---

[21] See RB 1.3. This, of course, stands in contrast to Benedict's own experience as described by Gregory, where he begins his monastic life as a hermit, a point not lost on many commentators of the Rule.

[22] *Regula Basilii*, Question 3:35, in *Rule of St Basil*, 81.

[23] See Cassian, *Conf.* 10.VII.1 (375–76).

PETER: I am led to deep and profound silence at these words. Is this truly wondrous transformation possible for us in this life, or must we wait for the life to come?

GREGORY: Indeed, we can experience a foretaste of this perfection in God, if even for a moment in time, when we pursue the virtuous life. And this must be our quest and aim always as we seek God in sincerity of heart.

10. So you see, Peter, the life at Nursia was like one continuous prayer.[24] Whether it be in their silent hours alone in prayer with the Scriptures; the hours of chanting the psalms together at morning, noon, evening, and night; whether it be as they went about their daily tasks; whether caring for the sick, feeding the poor, welcoming the strangers and travelers; or simply attending to the ordinary or menial chores of the house and estate, they always prayed to God that he would bring their work to completion through his love and mercy.[25]

Though Sophia guided her in the way of wisdom still, Scholastica governed the community, yet she considered herself the least of all those for whom she cared. This was evident in everything she did and everything she said. She always took her turn at cooking, cleaning, and working in the fields. She washed the feet of all the guests who came to their door, from the least to the greatest. And whenever there was an important decision to be made, she always gathered the community and took counsel with them. In this way she won the hearts of all.[26]

[24] See 1 Thess 5:17.
[25] See RB Prol. 4.
[26] See RB 3, "On Calling the Brothers for Counsel."

Chapter 8

Story of the Young Man, Justus

VIII. 1 PETER: The nature of this virtuous life is one that inspires imitation and is truly the way of the gospel.

GREGORY: This is true, Peter, but with the way of the gospel struggle and trial are often experienced. The cross is never far from those who truly seek God. Let me tell you now of one of Scholastica's most difficult struggles.

2. There was a young righteous man, named Justus, from the neighboring town, who, having heard of Scholastica's noble bearing and life of virtue, sought her out for counsel. So comely was this young man and so open to goodness and God's commands, that it soon became evident that the two were of one heart and mind. Indeed, a spiritual friendship grew between them. Throughout the village of Nursia they were often seen in holy conversation, or applying themselves to works of charity together. Justus was keen to learn the ways of wisdom and to devote his life to doing the Lord's will. He had often sat at the feet of holy hermits, but he also desired to live out his call to follow Christ in active love of his neighbor.

Justus had heard these words of the Gospel proclaimed: "Not everyone who says to me, 'Lord, Lord,' will enter the kingdom of heaven, but only the one who does the will of my Father in heaven,"[1] and, like Scholastica, had taken the gospel word into his heart. Yet the evil one, who is the enemy of all who are good, watched with impatience the great and growing virtue of Scholastica and saw here, in this spiritual friendship, an opening by which to try to discredit the blessed woman.[2] The wicked tongues of the envious and, before too long, the sordid thoughts of the depraved, spread malicious gossip about these two holy and righteous seekers of God.

3. So distressed was Scholastica about this vindictive talk that she sought the counsel of her spiritual mother, Sophia, and the local priest. This priest, however, was also trapped in the snares of the evil one, and had become jealous of Scholastica's fame and reputation for holiness. He accused her of seducing the good young man and corrupting his soul. And like the rapacious spread of a plague, the priest's evil words began to infect the whole town.

Sophia insisted that they pray together with the community for the guidance of the Holy Spirit in this grave matter. Sophia knew that Scholastica loved Justus with a pure and holy love, that they shared a spiritual friendship, and that this bond could not be broken through separation any more than the bond between Scholastica and her brother, the holy Benedict, could be severed.

4. Knowing that evil words breed evil actions, Sophia counseled Scholastica to go and plead with Justus to return to his own home and continue the Work of God there. But Justus, a good and upright man, had already contrived a

[1] Matt 7:21.
[2] This story parallels the struggles of Benedict; see *Dial.* II.VIII.1ff. (41ff.).

way to save Scholastica any further embarrassment.[3] He had himself made up his mind to continue back in his own village the good work that he and Scholastica had achieved in Nursia. Though this parting deeply saddened their hearts, they both understood the wisdom of their decisions. However, as guardians of each other's souls,[4] they would continue to strengthen their spiritual friendship through a constant stream of letters. Let me tell you, Peter, that this exchange of letters, just as that between Scholastica and her brother, enabled them to continue to share their hearts' desire for God and to grow stronger in their own bond of friendship.

5. PETER: Yet is it possible for such a friendship between a man and a woman to flourish?

GREGORY: Ah, Peter, it is a most natural arrangement for, as you will remember, woman and man were made by God as companions in this life.[5] And friendship is a gift from God, for where there is friendship there is God. We might even suggest that "those who remain in friendship remain in God and God in them."[6] This was truly so of Scholastica and Justus. Indeed, the source and origin of true spiritual friendship is love. For as we are told by the master, John Cassian, "For this is a properly ordered love, which

---

[3] An allusion to Joseph in Matt 1:19: "Her husband Joseph, being a righteous man and unwilling to expose her to public disgrace . . ."

[4] In Gregory's homily on John 15:12-16, he notes, "A friend can be called a kind of soul-keeper" (*Amicus enim quasi animi custos vocatur*). See *Homily* 27 (215).

[5] See the argument I have put on the lips of Gregory in the Prologue above, 2ff.

[6] See Aelred of Rievaulx, *Spiritual Friendship*, trans. Lawrence C. Braceland, ed. Marsha L. Dutton, Cistercian Fathers 5 (Collegeville, MN: Cistercian Publications, 2010), I.69-70 (65). I have taken the liberty of putting these words of Aelred on the lips of Gregory.

though hating no one, loves certain people more by reason of their good qualities. Although it loves everyone in a general way, nonetheless it makes an exception for itself of those whom it should embrace with a particular affection."[7]

Scholastica and Justus had laid a solid foundation for spiritual friendship, in that it began in Christ, continued with Christ, and was perfected in Christ.[8]

---

[7] See Cassian, *Conf.* 16:XIV.3 (565).
[8] *Spiritual Friendship*, I:10 (53).

Chapter 9

Scholastica Departs Nursia

IX. 1 Though Justus had departed of his own volition, the local priest in Nursia persisted in his loathsome envy of Scholastica. And it came to her hearing that the women in her community resented the old priest and the townsfolk for their envy and malicious talk concerning her. However, Scholastica's humility had grown greater through this evil experience of spite, and she upbraided the community for their idle talk and exhorted them to forgiveness of her accusers. Falling on her knees, Scholastica gazed up to heaven, crying, "Oh loving and sustaining God of all creation, you know of all things even before they have come to pass, for nothing is hidden from you. You delivered Susanna from her false accusers because she trusted in you. Grant that through your mercy this community, here gathered together in your name, may know freedom from all hateful scandal that comes from the evil one."[1]

2. She could see that her presence was causing hardship and a lack of peace to her community of sisters. Not only this, but it was also no longer possible to house the growing community on her father's estate, and she was at a loss as

[1] See *Life of Saint Leoba*, 217.

to what to do next. So it happened that not long after Justus left, Scholastica gathered her community, now large in number, for counsel, and together they prayed and fasted for three days, singing psalms and invoking the Lord's name. As they persevered in prayer and discernment, it was upon the youngest member of the community that the Spirit rested, and it was from her that the wisdom of God came flowing forth.[2] Prudentia, of tender years, stood in their midst and declared that perhaps it was better for some of them to leave this place in order to spread the goodness of God that they had found there. All were moved by her simple and profound words, and yet, at the same time, they were also challenged by their wisdom.

3. Loading a cart with supplies for the journey, Scholastica and twelve of the sisters, with Prudentia among them, set off on their way. They departed her beloved home in Nursia for a place that God would show them, and left her old and faithful teacher, Sophia, responsible for the vibrant community remaining on the family property.

Like Christ with his twelve apostles, Scholastica traveled south, not knowing exactly where they were to end up but trusting in God's providence. For a time they felt like wandering Aramaeans, but girded with faith and the performance of good works, they hoped in a promised land for themselves.[3] With the psalms as their constant song and the gospel as their guide, they set out on their way, mindful of God's call to his kingdom.[4]

---

[2] See RB 3.3.
[3] See RB Prol. 21.
[4] See RB Prol. 21.

Chapter 10

The Wounded Goth

X. 1 During this time, Peter, as I have already told you, the whole of Italy was overrun by Goths who were of the Arian conviction. So, the journey from Nursia was not an easy one for Scholastica and her sisters. Some days they found themselves on the road with many rough and violent soldiers of the Arian King Totila.[1]

However, Scholastica's serene and noble demeanor, and the way she encouraged her sisters to be bold yet gentle in the response to the many hostile insults and jeers towards them as they continued on their way, frequently averted what could have otherwise been a violent attack on their gentle nature. Miraculously, they remained untainted by any of these confrontations, and their prayers for their enemies and for peace in the land were heard throughout the countryside as they continued their singing of psalms and hymns throughout the day and night.

2. One day they happened upon a wounded Goth lying beside the road, Otrain by name, who, being near death, had been cruelly abandoned by his regiment. Though the

[1] Totila, a significant general of the time, reigned over the Ostrogoths from 541 to 552. He plays an important role in Benedict's story also. See *Dial.* II.XIV–XV (62–63).

sisters were afraid of him, Scholastica, her heart full of compassion, immediately approached the injured man. Having requested of him his name, she politely asked him if he would allow her and the sisters to give him what aid was in their power, aware that his dignity may be affronted by receiving help from mere women.

Otrain was overcome by Blessed Scholastica's fearless and kind offer of mercy to an enemy. He cried out to her that he was a sinful and violent man, unworthy of her help, and had been so all his life.[2] He deserved to die there on the side of the road. She should pass by and pay no heed to his worthless soul. Scholastica smiled lovingly at Otrain, got down on her knees beside him, and gently began to remove his armor in order to attend more easily to his wounds. She ordered the sisters to bring to her some soothing oil, food, and refreshing water for Otrain.[3] At this Odiata, a younger sister of the company, became very distressed and anxious.[4] She came forward and pleaded with Scholastica: "Holy Mother, we have barely enough food and water for ourselves. If we are to share it with this dangerous and evil man, we will not have enough to continue on our journey. Aside from this, he is already as good as dead, and he is a heretic, an Arian who would, if he could, do us great harm in both body and spirit! Do you not care for our safety in these troubled times?"

3. Scholastica, who was by now gently cradling the wounded soldier's head on her lap, turned and, looking intently at Odiata, she reached out one of her hands to the young sister, held it firmly, and said, "Do you see this man, Odiata? He has been left dying by the side of the road. Does

[2] See Luke 5:8.
[3] See the parable of the Good Samaritan, Luke 10:25-37.
[4] A play on the Latin, *odium*—hatred.

he not look to you as if he is in need? Do not the gospel words, 'Who is my neighbor,' come flooding into your heart when you look at him in this condition? Do you not feel Christ's call to imitate the actions of the kind Samaritan on the road to Jericho? Or do you wish to act as the Levite or the priest in this story, and walk on by this distressed soul?" Looking back at the wounded Otrain, she asked Odiata: "Tell us, Odiata, what must we do? Are we to love this man as Christ has taught us, or are we to pass on by?" With tears of compunction welling up in her eyes, Odiata found herself also down on her knees, begging forgiveness from the wounded Otrain.

4. Scholastica spoke then to the other sisters: "My dearest sisters, we are called to prefer Christ above all else,[5] and here in this man, Otrain—a stranger—we have before us the face of Christ. Do you not believe this? And so, we must welcome him as Christ."[6] At these wise words, the sisters brought what they had from their cart to minister healing to the soldier who had been their enemy and was now their brother in Christ. Odiata for her part never left Otrain's side from that moment on, praying for his recovery and ministering to his wounds with all gentleness and compassion.

5. Together, they made room for the soldier in the back of their cart, and carefully laid him there so that they could continue on their way. Though this caused the sisters much hardship as they traveled, they took this yoke upon themselves together and they came to see their burden as light,[7] and the joy in their hearts increased.

[5] See RB 4.21.
[6] See RB 53.1.
[7] See Matt 11:28-30.

When they reached the next town they sought refuge not just for themselves but also for the wounded Otrain. Weary from their journey, they stayed there for some time, and to the amazement of the villagers they nursed this heretic Arian soldier back to the vigor of health. In reply to the wariness and concern of the people of the town, they preached the message of the Gospels to them, announcing the words of Jesus—that you must love your enemies and do good to those who persecute you, bless those who curse you and pray for those who mistreat you.[8] So astounded at the faith of these holy women, the people of the town aided them in their care of Otrain and also began to gather with Scholastica and her sisters as they sang their morning and evening songs of praise, thanking God for the gift of these women's wisdom among them.

6. It was this one voice of worship, along with all their attentive and loving care, that eventually soothed Otrain's violent temperament and softened his heart. And it was Scholastica's and Odiata's gentle words about the love of Christ that gradually brought Otrain to believe in the true nature of Christ, "begotten and not made, true God from true God, one in being with the Father."[9] This miracle of conversion ought not to be underestimated, Peter, for the power of the gospel is often made manifest in weakness, and the example of Christ's love is a much greater weapon of conversion than are the words of the mighty.[10]

Otrain, for his part, decided to devote his life to the protection of the sisters and continued with them along their difficult journey. He was of great assistance and comfort to

[8] See Luke 6:27-28.

[9] I have Gregory quote the Nicene Creed here to stress the orthodox belief in the face of the sisters' confrontation with Arianism.

[10] See 2 Cor 12:9.

them in times of need, building them shelters when there was no town to house them and finding them provisions when hunger or thirst assailed them.

7. PETER: Scholastica and her sisters proved themselves not only truly brave in their actions but steadfast in their faith.

GREGORY: You have perceived this rightly, Peter. God's commandments enjoin us to love our neighbors as ourselves; and, seeing that we are charged to love them with this depth of charity, how much more ought we to assist them by catering to their physical needs in order that we might relieve their misery, if not in all the particulars of their life, then at least by some measure of support. So whenever we find someone who is in distress of any kind, be that from grievous wounds of mind or body, and an inability to manage, or from lack of food, clothing, or shelter, we are impelled, as far as it is in our means, to arrange care for them.[11] And when we perceive error, to gently bring them, not by coercion or force, but by example and charity, to that love of Christ which leads us to the perfection of God. As Christ said, "be perfect, therefore, as your heavenly Father is perfect."[12] And this perfection is simply this: That we love one another as Christ has loved us. This is, indeed, how we are known as Christ's disciples.[13]

8. PETER: This command of love to which we aspire is a fearsome thing and demanding of all we do in our life.

---

[11] In this section I am drawing on the text of Gregory the Great's letter 1.44 to Peter the Subdeacon. See *The Letters of Gregory the Great*, Vol. 1, trans. John R. C. Martyn (Toronto: Pontifical Institute of Mediaeval Studies, 2004), 170.

[12] Matt 5:48.

[13] See John 13:34-35.

GREGORY: Yes, Peter. "What should we take God's law to mean in this context but charity, since it is through charity that we always keep the commandments of life in mind, in the sense that they are followed by action? The voice of Truth speaks of this law as follows: 'This is my commandment, that you love one another.'[14] Paul chimes in: 'Love is the fullness of the law.'[15] Elsewhere he says, 'Bear one another's burdens, and in this way, you will fulfill Christ's law.'[16] And what can be more fittingly understood by Christ's law than love, which we perfectly fulfill when we carry a neighbor's load out of love?

This law is called complex because charity reaches out eagerly and anxiously for all virtuous acts. Charity takes its cue, certainly, from two commandments, but it reaches out to perform innumerable actions. Love of God, you see, and love of neighbor are the beginning of this law.

9. Without question Paul describes the great variety of this law when he says, 'Charity is patient and kind; she is not envious or boastful, she is not depraved or scheming, nor is she self-seeking, she is not irritable; she thinks no evil; she does not rejoice over wickedness but rejoices with the truth.'[17] Of course, charity is patient, because she endures the bad things that are done to her with equanimity. She is kind because she freely bestows good for evil. She is not envious, because she has no desire for the things of this world, and so she cannot envy any worldly success. She is not boastful, because when she anxiously desires the reward of interior recompense, she does not exult over exterior possessions. She is not depraved, because only love of God

[14] John 15:12.
[15] Rom 13:10.
[16] Gal 6:2.
[17] See 1 Cor 13:4-6.

and neighbor excites her, and she has nothing to do with any departure from rectitude. She is not a schemer, because she ardently pursues her own interior interests, so she by no means desires another's exterior possessions. She is not self-seeking, because whatever transitory possessions she has here below she neglects, as though they belonged to someone else; she recognizes nothing as belonging to herself except that which remains close to her.

She is not irritable, because even when she receives an injury she is not provoked or moved to self-defense, and she hopes for a greater reward hereafter for her grave troubles here. She thinks no evil, because she secures her mind with the love of purity and she roots out all hatred from herself, so she cannot allow anything impure in her soul. She does not rejoice over wickedness, because she desires to have only love toward all, so she does not even exult at the discomfiture of an adversary. She rejoices with the truth, because when she loves other people as herself, seeing their rectitude, she becomes happy as though it were by the advancement of her own interests."[18]

10. So you can see, Peter, that this law of God has many aspects to which we must aspire with all our heart, our mind, our will, and our strength. But let us return to our story so as to observe how these aspects of love are embodied in this account of the life of holy Scholastica.

[18] In this long section, I have drawn directly from Gregory's *Moralia on Job*, Book X, VI:7-8 and 10, because of the profound beauty of the text itself at this point. See Gregory the Great, *Moral Reflections on the Book of Job*, vol. 2, 340, 345–46.

Chapter 11

Scholastica Visits Her
Brother Benedict

XI. 1 With Otrain as their companion and protector, Scholastica and the sisters now felt more at ease on their dangerous journey. Indeed, their fear grew more and more into a gentle love towards those they met along the way, sharing what food they possessed and never finding themselves without a welcoming shelter in the towns they passed through. Such was their confidence in Christ's presence among them that, like the lilies of the field, they worried neither about what they were to eat or drink or about themselves and their attire, for as Christ himself states, "Is not life more than food, and the body more than clothing?"[1]

2. Now it happened that Scholastica came to hear that her brother Benedict had taken on the care of a community of monks at Vicovaro. This news left her feeling somewhat uneasy, and she had a dream that caused her great distress. In this dream all the bells in all the churches of the towns of Italy broke into a million pieces and ceased to ring out their praise of God to the world. Although she prayed that her anxiety for her brother would cease, she could not turn

---

[1] Matt 6:25; and see 6:28.

her mind to their present journey, so she decided to consult her sisters again on what she should do about this lack of peace in her heart. Together, they spent the whole day in prayer and fasting, while Otrain sought shelter for them in a nearby village. Scholastica's three closest friends and faithful advisers spoke first. Fidelia counseled that she pray for faith in God's will and that eventually all would be well for her brother. Speranza encouraged her to put her hope in God's merciful providence. But it was Desideria who insisted that love should impel Scholastica to act and visit her brother in what could well be his time of greatest need.

3. PETER: I must admit that I am curious at this point. Is this not the third time you have related to me how Scholastica sought counsel from others: twice before she left her home in Nursia and now at this juncture of their journey?

GREGORY: Yes, Peter, it is good that you have noticed this quality in Scholastica, for you should take heed of this wisdom in your own life. A wise leader will always seek the advice of those they serve on important issues and ponder this counsel before they come to a decision.[2] Remember where it is written: "Do all things with counsel, and afterward you will have nothing to regret."[3] This is the path of discernment that we should all live in this life, Peter. When we listen deeply to the stirrings of the Spirit in others as well as in ourselves, God often allows us to hear the voice of Wisdom herself, even when that wisdom comes from the most unexpected places, as we have already seen in this story of Blessed Scholastica. In our present example, Scholastica shows us in her sober discernment what the

[2] See RB 3, "On Calling the Brothers for Counsel." In this section Benedict outlines the manner in which the abbot consults the monks on all serious matters in the monastery.

[3] See Sir 32:24 and RB 3.13.

Apostle tells us is to "belong to the day," as she put on the breastplate of faith and love, and for a helmet she wore the hope of salvation.[4]

PETER: This is indeed deep wisdom shining through the character of a woman. But do continue with the tale, for I am anxious to know if Scholastica finally meets with Benedict after his terrible time at Vicovaro.

4. GREGORY: I will indeed continue with this tale of wisdom for you, Peter, for there is still much to tell. All the sisters were agreed that, as Vicovaro was only a short distance from them, they would visit Scholastica's esteemed brother. They added that not only would Scholastica be relieved of her inner burden but that they, along with Otrain, would surely profit from such a visit to the wise and holy Benedict, who had forsaken the world in order to seek God.

Upon receiving a very cold reception from the brothers at Vicovaro, the sisters learned that Benedict had retired, alone, back to his isolated cave. Scholastica was even more distressed, and so they traveled the short distance to Subiaco, only to find the blessed Benedict sitting rather troubled and despondent outside his cave on the mountainside. Remember, Peter, how I related to you the story of these wicked monks of Vicovaro and their resistance to Benedict's zeal for reform of their monastery.[5]

PETER: Indeed, I do! I was shocked at the way the brothers, having asked Benedict for help, then tried to poison the man of God's wine. I also marveled at the way Benedict's blessing shattered the cup and saved him from drinking the evil done by this wicked and recalcitrant community.

---

[4] See 1 Thess 5:8.
[5] *Dial.* II.III:3ff. (21ff.).

GREGORY: Well done, Peter, you have indeed remembered this tragic story. Nevertheless, there was still more that Benedict needed to learn about the true nature of wisdom.

5. Here outside the cave, Scholastica and Benedict embraced and greeted each other with a holy kiss. After some time, explaining her presence there, the wise Scholastica who now sat beside her brother leaned towards him with deep concern and asked, "What are these rumors that I have heard spread about you, my dearest brother? What have you done, that so much discord reigns in this community of brothers at Vicovaro?[6] Why are they not of one heart and mind? And why have you returned to this lonely place?" The man of God, Benedict, related his story to his holy sister as she listened intently. Together they talked of the community's reluctance to be reformed by Benedict's rigorous application of discipline and the dreadful end that then ensued.

6. "What experience and wise guidance did you yourself use in instructing the brothers in this path, dearest brother?" asked Blessed Scholastica with some trepidation. Blessed Benedict then showed his curious sister the old book of rules that he had found in the community itself, and he talked of how he had failed to implement these same rules with the monks of Vicovaro. So together they read these rules, and as they read, Scholastica was more and more troubled by what she heard, for these rules, so wise in essentials, were yet often lacking discretion, moderation, and

[6] I have created a contrasting parallel here. In the *Life of Benedict*, it is Benedict who exclaims, "What have you done?" when, at their final meeting, Scholastica's prayers are answered by God in direct contradiction to Benedict's will. See *Dial.* II.XXXIII.4 (124).

most of all, charity. Indeed, the leader of the community was advised to be oversuspicious and so strict in his punishment of the monks as to have surely instilled no peace in the brethren at all.[7] The rules were, indeed, harsh and burdensome, and left her feeling that they gave no hope of experiencing the joys of heaven, which she herself had known so often in her own community. "Did you discuss these rules with the brothers or attempt to adjust them to this community with all their weaknesses, my brother?" asked Scholastica gently. "No," replied Benedict, "these rules looked venerable enough to me, and I trusted in the discipline that they would inspire."

"Yet," countered the wise Scholastica, "in your adherence to them without counsel, have these rules not led you to this reputation for harshness and unreasonable demands, instead of the wisdom of charitable moderation and holy discretion in your dealings with this community which you led? Had you but guided them with love and example, surely they would not have sought to be rid of you."[8] It was clear to Scholastica that the monks feared Benedict and his rigorous and zealous discipline, and had not learned to love him as their shepherd.

7. But Benedict protested: "We are men, my dear sister, not weak and gentle women as you have led. We need more solid and rigorous words to guide us in our manly desire for God." At this demeaning rebuke, Scholastica was indignant and sternly reminded him: "Surely, we are one in Christ Jesus, my brother, in both flesh and in spirit. As the Apostle proclaims: 'There is no longer Jew or Greek, there is no longer slave or free, there is no longer male and female;

---

[7] See the contrast with qualities of the abbot, all of which lead to peace in RB 64.16.

[8] See RB 2.12.

for all of you are one in Christ Jesus."[9] You, my dearest brother, as leader of the community, take the place of Christ in the midst of the brothers,[10] but this means you must strive all the harder to be loved by them, rather than feared.[11] It is not the weakness of women you need concern yourself with, but the weakness of men!" And finally she dared to instruct him: "Temper your zeal, my brother, and perhaps you will understand this weakness and be the wiser for it. These are beloved souls of God that you are commanded to shepherd. You must hate the vices of those you love, and yet put mercy before judgment in your care of them. I have learned from years in community and through hard experience to act with prudence and without excessive correction, so as not to bend the bruised reed or give cause for grumbling within the community.[12] Don't you think you might soften their hearts with love and compassion and then lead them gently all together along the way of God's commands?"

8. Then Benedict, head bowed and somewhat chastened, replied, "Oh, forgive my infelicity towards you, learned and venerable sister." And he admitted: "I see now that you are so thoroughly taught by wisdom, though perhaps I did need to be a little harsh to begin with. These are, after all, crude men. But I truly did try to do as you say—to lead by love and example. Nevertheless, these brothers do not seek God but their own will and base desires. They do not want a leader or a rule to guide them on the paths of God's righteousness and justice, and so I have abandoned them to their own evil intentions. Your words rightly humbled my

---

[9] Gal 3:28.
[10] See RB 2.2.
[11] See RB 64.15.
[12] I have taken most of this section from RB 64.

heart and mind. Let us talk longer of this rule and how, with the way of wisdom and discretion, we might together moderate its rigor so that it could be an apt guide for those who truly seek God."

9. So, in that lonely cave, the saintly siblings knelt and prayed together for the Spirit's guidance in these matters. Ever so lovingly and gently, Scholastica talked to her zealous brother about ways that he might bring a community to love him rather than fear him.[13] She counseled him to give the strong of the community something to strive for, and the weak nothing to run from, through his compassion and solicitous care of them rather than through any strict adherence to law.[14] She counseled him in this way: "Not all can be as zealous as you, dearest brother, in their striving to please God, even as they long to know God. You must give them all something to hope for as they all make this journey to loving one another in obedience. In this way, by explaining that although the road to life may be narrow at first and, as you insist, a little strictness may be necessary to begin with, eventually this same narrow road will open on to an unspeakable joy of running the way of God's commandments."[15] And she added by way of ending her advice, "Indeed, dearest brother, it is not the iron rod of law and discipline, but love that brings the wretched soul to desire the will of God."

10. Scholastica and her sisters spent some time at Subiaco with Benedict, but soon it was time for them to move on in their journey to find a suitable permanent home for establishing their mission of charity. And it was not long

[13] See RB 64.15.
[14] See RB 64.19.
[15] See RB Prol. 49.

after this visit that Benedict left his cave to form a community of monks at Subiaco. You have heard about this, Peter, in our previous conversation.[16]

And so it is that where the light shines forth you can see that there is often a darkness that tries to cover its revealing brightness, but as the Evangelist tells us, "What has come into being in him was life, and the life was the light of all people. The light shines in the darkness, and the darkness did not overcome it."[17] Scholastica and Benedict knew this light in the dark moments of their seeking of God. But let me not be distracted in the telling of this tale of Scholastica and her sisters.

[16] See *Dial.* II.III.14 (31).
[17] John 1:3-5.

Chapter 12

Scholastica Allays the
Fears of a Village

XII. 1 On one occasion as the holy women of God continued on their arduous journey, a terrible storm began to
grow in strength and ferocity all around them. Even with
the help of Otrain they were finding it impossible to make
any significant progress against such a mighty wind whirl-
ing about their ears and a driving rain soaking them to the
bone. So they sought refuge from the appalling conditions
in a small village which they came to in due course.

2. In the village there was a local priest, a kindly soul,
who was only too pleased to welcome them and give them
sanctuary from the storm in his humble church, although
he feared it would not be enough to save any of them against
such a mighty gale. Yet, here in this little wooden church,
they spent their time in prayer together throughout the night
of this terrible and raging tempest.[1] As the storm worsened,
the threatening thunder caused the earth to quake, bolts of
lightning lit up the night sky, and the merciless wind rocked

[1] This story is based on a similar incident found in *Life of Saint Leoba*,
219, thus setting the stage for Scholastica to be the precursor model of
Christ for such stories.

the very foundations of all the little dwellings of the village, including the small and humble church. In truth, it threatened to cast the entire village into the abyss.

3. Now the jealousy of the evil one had continued to follow Scholastica and her sisters from Nursia, so that the townsfolk came to believe this terror had been brought upon them by this peculiar band of wandering women from an unknown place in the north. Besides which, they were traveling with a strange and fearsome looking Goth who was surely ungodly and possessed of an evil spirit.

The villagers hurried to the little church, intending to curse the women, but here they found Blessed Scholastica and her sisters praying fervently before the altar of God. Indeed, they were incredulous, as it appeared to them that Scholastica, whose weary head was lying on the shoulder of the Goth, had fallen asleep in prayer and did not seem to have noticed them or the fury of the storm that assailed them.[2] Struck with awe at her seeming indifference, they cried out in a great fear: "Why have you brought this judgment of God upon us? Are we all to die because of you?" At this moment the sisters also became frightened and agitated. Prudentia, who knew that holy Scholastica was full of faith and wisdom, appealed to her, saying, "Holy Mother, awake, for we are in peril. All hope for us and these poor distressed villagers depends on your prayer. Intercede with Christ for us now, or we will all perish."

4. At this outcry, Blessed Scholastica opened her eyes, lifted her head, and said to Prudentia and her cowering sisters, "Why are you afraid? Have you no faith?" With that, she calmly got up from her knees and invited the crowd to be patient and of sure hope. The holy woman, Scholastica,

[2] See Mark 4:35-41.

exhorted the villagers to join her and the sisters in heartfelt prayer to God before the altar. But the horrified townsfolk were unable to contain their panic as the storm continued to shake the walls of the little church and the ground on which they stood. Their cries would not cease, and as the holy one looked steadily at them all, their tears moved her to compassion for them, and in her heart she yearned for them to be at peace.

5. Thus it was that Scholastica ceased from her prayers and tossed away the cloak she was wearing to shield her from the wind and rain. With only Christ as her protection, she took the large cross from the altar and moved through the people to the doors of the church and flung them open. Holding the cross aloft in front of the oncoming wind and rain, she made the sign of the cross with it, held out her arms and prayed in a loud voice into the howling wind: "*Kyrie eleison, Christe eleison, Kyrie eleison*: Lord have mercy, Christ have mercy, Lord have mercy." And, filled with awe and terror, all the sisters, the priest, and the people repeated the words after her. Then almost immediately the storm was stilled, the rain ceased, the wind died down, the thunder was silent, and the lightning was no more. Gradually the darkness was no longer dark, and the light of the moon and the stars shone all around them in peaceful tranquility.[3] What remained was only "a sound of sheer silence."[4]

The people stood there in amazement and wonder, while Scholastica turned to them and said, "Why is it that you do not trust in God's love and care for you? Why is it that you were afraid? Be of good faith and you will know God's peace always in your hearts." And they all knelt in

[3] See John 1:5.
[4] See 1 Kgs 19:11-12. The sheer silence denotes the presence of God in the story of Elijah on the mountain.

astonishment at the mighty works God had performed through a woman. From that day on the town became known throughout the area for its joy in believing in the mercy of God.

6. PETER: This is truly an amazing and miraculous story, for surely it heralds the embodiment of Christ in the life of Blessed Scholastica.

GREGORY: All saints are embodiments of Christ, Peter, for they model what St. Paul says in his letter to the Galatians: "It is no longer I who live, but it is Christ who lives in me. And the life I now live in the flesh I live by faith in the Son of God, who loved me and gave himself for me."[5]

It was Blessed Scholastica's insistence that one should never lose hope in God's mercy that enabled her to call forth this miracle of mercy.[6] Let me tell you of another such tale about this holy woman and her valiant belief in the merciful compassion of God, as it should not go unheard in the telling of her story.

[5] Gal 2:20.
[6] See RB 4.74, the final in St. Benedict's list of the tools of good works necessary for the monastic life.

Chapter 13

Scholastica Pleads for the Life of Prisoners

XIII. 1 The sisters stayed in that village for only a short time to comfort the people with their prayers and good works. Indeed, some of the young women of the town decided to join the sisters in their holy endeavor, and so the little company found that they were growing in number. Like a tree planted beside streams of living water, they were slowly but surely yielding fruit of a sweet flavor.[1] However, after some time they discerned together that this was not a suitable site for them to make their home, as there was not enough food or water to sustain them and the village's community as well. Thus they decided it was God's will that they move on.

Traveling the roads at this time brought its own dangers, as I have already pointed out to you, Peter, and Blessed Scholastica and her sisters were not always spared these dangers. I will tell of just one occasion that was related to me about how they were able, with God's help, to bring some portion of peace to a troubled land.

[1] See Ps 1:3.

2. On one bright and sunny morning, after the sisters had sung their morning offering and had set off on their journey, Otrain suddenly halted, and a look of overwhelming terror came upon his face. The holy Scholastica asked Otrain what it was that distressed him so. The former soldier pointed to a rise in the road in front of them, where there was a small camp of soldiers outside the ancient walled town of Ferentino.[2] Immediately, not thinking first of her own safety or that of the sisters, Scholastica realized that if the camp were of orthodox believers, Otrain, clearly a Goth, would be in danger, and if it were a camp of Arian soldiers he would also be in peril as a deserter. Turning to the sisters, she exhorted them, "Fear not!" And she bravely proclaimed, "for we are all believers in the one God of our Lord Jesus Christ who is our sure armor and shield so that we may be able to stand against the wiles of the devil. As Scripture tells us, 'our struggle is not against enemies of blood and flesh, but against the rulers, against the authorities, against the cosmic powers of this present darkness, against the spiritual forces of evil in the heavenly places.'[3] Faith will be our shield, hope our breastplate, and love—our message of peace—will be our sword." And making the sign of the cross, she led them forth.

3. Thus it was that Blessed Scholastica and her company came to a small camp of soldiers who were blocking their path. These men belonged to the general John the Sanguinary,[4] and though of orthodox faith, were known

---

[2] Ferentino is located 65 km southeast of Rome on the road to Naples and about 73 km from Monte Cassino. Its history dates back to pre-Roman times. See Biancamaria Valeri, *Ferentino sfumature di luce e storia* (Rome: Dantebus Edizioni, 2022).

[3] Eph 6:11-12.

[4] "John the Sanguinary," named for his bloody campaigns, was a Roman general under Justinian I. See Procopius, *The Anecdota or Secret History*, Vol. 6, trans. Henry Bronson Dewing, Loeb Classical Library

for their merciless and bloody confrontations with the Arian troops. With them were three prisoners who were clearly beaten to the point of death. Appalled by the sight of their wretched condition, Odiata was moved to pity and ran immediately towards them, but was blocked by spears and the jeering of the soldiers.

The captain of the camp, Eleos by name, came forward to address them.[5] "What strange company do we have here in our midst? Indeed, what is it that you fair and frail women are doing on the road, for it is clear to me that you are not where you belong in these dangerous times." Pointing at Otrain, he added, "And who, pray tell, is this heretic—a Goth, no less—a sworn enemy of our kin—that you have in your company? Why is it that you travel together, and where is it that you are headed?"

4. Blessed Scholastica stepped forward and without fear in her voice announced: "We are women of God, commanded by the Lord to do his works of charity and prayer wherever they are needed. We travel in order to find a safe and peaceful place where we can continue our work of charity to our neighbor and remain undisturbed in our praise and worship of the One True God of Christ Jesus our Lord and Savior." Then turning to Otrain, she boldly exclaimed, "And Otrain, this Goth, whom you see and despise, is newly come to conversion and the understanding of the true nature of Christ. He, of his own volition, aids and protects us in our desire to work for God's mission." Without hesitating, she then pointed in the direction in which Odiata had run, and she boldly demanded: "These poor souls whom you have beaten mercilessly—you will release them into our

---

(Cambridge, MA: Harvard University Press, 1960); and Peter Heather, *Rome Resurgent: War and Empire in the Age of Justinian* (Oxford: Oxford University Press, 2018).

[5] Eleos, the Greek word for mercy, clemency, compassion, and pity.

care, and you will let us proceed on our way without further delay."

5. With a bearing of utter disdain, Eleos declared to Scholastica, "Dearest sister in the Lord, do you realize that I have the power to end your lives here and now without hesitation or concern?" Holy Scholastica moved closer still and, without any sign of fear, looked deeply into Eleos's heart and replied, "Noble Eleos, of even nobler name, do you not realize that I have the power to allow you to end our lives here and now without hesitation or concern? You have no power over us other than that given you from above."[6] Then she added a warning to him: "Would you then dare to interfere with the works of God?"

In wonder at the valiant courage and firm faith of this holy woman, the great warrior Eleos stepped back in utter amazement, as if being assailed by a fearless foe. He was so impressed with Blessed Scholastica's strength of character and dignified presence that his heart was softened towards her.[7] "Would you not sit and rest awhile with us, Holy Mother, and tell us of how you have come to such faith as to command the mercy of a powerful army?"

6. Without shifting her steady gaze from Eleos, Scholastica continued to question him further: "Do not the holy Scriptures, which we both revere, exhort us to love our enemies and do good to those who persecute us?[8] Do you not believe these words of the Son of God, our Lord and Savior Jesus Christ? Are you not bound by these words—the Word of God—in all that you do?"

At this Eleos became afraid of Blessed Scholastica, but, reading his heart, she again leaned toward him and gently

[6] See John 19:11.
[7] See *Life of St Radegunde by the Nun, Baudonivia*, 385.
[8] See Luke 6:27-28.

pleaded with him: "If you truly believe all that Christ has taught us, allow us to tend to your prisoners with what ointments we have, and, being true to your name, set them free into our merciful care.[9] We will see that they neither come to any harm nor do anyone harm."

7. Growing increasingly puzzled by the persistence of this strange woman, Eleos replied, "They ought to die, yet you would bother with them?"

And immediately Scholastica assured him: "We will care for them and bring them to the knowledge of the true faith if you but hand them over to us. We will take them with us on our journey wherever it is that God is leading us, and because of your mercy they will become prisoners of Christ and messengers of peace."

Unable to resist the firm, yet compassionate and pene-trating gaze of Scholastica, Eleos instructed his soldiers to let Odiata pass through to the prisoners in order to minister to them. He then provided Otrain a cart onto which he commanded his soldier to load the wounded prisoners. Then he turned, and facing the holy woman of God, asked for her blessing on his immortal soul and those of his com-pany so that they may place mercy above judgment in all their actions and not forget the faith for which they fought.

8. PETER: Truly, the Spirit of courage and fortitude was with Scholastica and her little company.

GREGORY: As our hearts expand, dear Peter, so too does our desire to bring Christ's message of peace to our world. So Scholastica and her growing company continued, unimpeded, on their way, and were eventually to find a place where they could finally put down roots for their life together. Now let me relate to you how this came about.

[9] See Luke 4:18.

Chapter 14

Establishing a Home in Cassino

XIV. 1 As time passed, Scholastica and the sisters came to the small village of Cassino at the foot of a mountain overlooking a wide valley.[1] Remember, Peter, this is the mountain that Benedict eventually settled on, and you will hear how it was holy Scholastica's wisdom that drew him there.[2]

Here they found the local people to be hospitable but still adhering to the worship of the Greek god, Apollo. This was a source of great anxiety to many of Scholastica's sisters, and one of them exhorted her to ask Otrain and his three brothers, now healed and instructed in the faith, to go and smash the idols that the local people gathered around in strange acts of unseemly worship.[3] But the blessed Scholastica counseled peace, and suggested that Otrain and the

---

[1] Cassino, or *Casinum*, was an ancient town in central Italy. For details of its history see Tommaso Leccisotti, *Monte Cassino*, trans. Armand O. Citarella (Abbey of Monte Cassino, 1987). See Prologue, footnote 6.

[2] *Dial.* II.VIII.10 (49).

[3] The smashing of idols or sacred symbols of indigenous peoples is common in ancient hagiography; for example, see *Life of Radegunde*, 403, and also *Life of Boniface*. See Willibald, *The Life of St. Boniface*, in *The Anglo-Saxon Missionaries in Germany: Being the Lives of SS. Willibrord, Boniface, Sturm, Leoba, and Lebuin, Together with the Hodoeporicon of*

others might be better employed with building them a shelter than with destroying useless objects. She instructed them that it would be through their words and actions, not by any violent persuasion or through their judgment or condemnation, that the way of God's love would be made known to these people.

2. Thus it was that having established a home for themselves, the sisters settled into a regular pattern of life. They divided their day between regular hours of prayer, tending their own gardens, and holy reading. They also set about caring for the sick and aged of the village. They shared what they had with the poor of the town and slowly got to know the people, their ways, and their beliefs. Through welcoming them to their prayers and to their table, Scholastica's companions discovered a people gentle and open both to their ministrations and to hearing of the freedom of the gospel. Indeed, the people came to love the sisters, and built for them a small hermitage halfway up the mountain in honor of St. Thecla, so that Scholastica and the other sisters might have a place of solitude and prayer, away from the many cares that otherwise occupied their lives.[4]

St. Willibald and a Selection from the Correspondence of St. Boniface, trans. Charles H. Talbot (New York: Sheed and Ward, 1954), 45–46.

[4] Schuster gives details of a "small house" not far from the monastery where Scholastica and Benedict used to meet. By establishing Scholastica's hermitage, I have adjusted this location for my own purposes. See Schuster, *St. Benedict and His Times,* 341.

Chapter 15

Benedict's Troubles and His Move to Monte Cassino

XV. 1 After some time passed, Benedict wrote to his esteemed and beloved sister, describing his initial success with forming communities at Subiaco and the joy that this had given him, due in no mean part to her wise counsel when she had been with him. Yet he also revealed to her the continuing and canny wiles of the devil, who did not cease from attacking the goodness of his community. For the success of one, though it ought to bring great joy to all, can often lead to envy in the souls of others whose hearts are not pure and who do not hope in God alone. Yes, Peter, the destructive force of the demon of jealousy haunts the fickle human heart and brings much sorrow and woe. You have already heard me speak of Benedict's sadness in Subiaco at not finding the peace that leads to life.[1] His one desire was for a place where the brothers could truly be free to continue their search for God in stillness and tranquility of heart.

2. Filled with discretion, the mother of all virtues,[2] Scholastica replied to Benedict, suggesting that he bring his

[1] *Dial.* II.VIII.1ff. (41ff.).
[2] See RB 64.19.

faithful followers to Cassino. There on the mount, long abandoned by idol worshippers as she described it to him, was a place of deep silence and freedom to seek God and pursue peace; a place where springs of living water could be gathered into the heart of those who desire Christ above all else.

On hearing about this blessed site, together with Scholastica's counsel, Benedict immediately packed up his community and made the journey south so as to establish his monastery on the summit of Monte Cassino. And this story you have heard in full.

Chapter 16

The Meetings of Scholastica and Benedict at Monte Cassino

XVI. 1 As I have told you, Peter, every year Benedict and Scholastica used to meet for prayer and holy conversation. It was during Lent that Scholastica and her companions would go about the town of Cassino distributing alms to the poor, attending to the sick, and praying for peace in the land. During this time, Benedict would come down from the monastery and there he would find his sister waiting for him in her little hermitage on the mountainside. He would be loaded with goods which Scholastica could use for her good works, and with a book for her to refresh her own spirit and that of her sisters. Though there were many such meetings, I will tell you about just two of them as I have heard about them from Fidelia, Speranza, and Desideria, who used to attend to the needs of the holy pair during these meetings.

Chapter 17

A Lesson in Obedience

XVII. 1 At one time a younger sister of Scholastica's community, Sinceria by name, disturbed their converse with an urgent request to speak to the blessed Mother. Scholastica was a little annoyed at being deprived of her intimate and precious time of dialogue with her brother. Nevertheless, in light of Sinceria's insistence, she granted her admittance to their holy space.

"Gracious Mother," she cried, "I have come because you had informed me this morning that I am to go tomorrow with Sister Fidelia to minister at Plumbariola and to live with the sisters there." In truth, Scholastica had established a small community of sisters in this town not far from Cassino.[1]

"Yes, this is my wish," replied Scholastica sternly, "and under holy obedience you must go as you are bidden." At this harsh response from Scholastica, Sinceria, with tears beginning to fall from her eyes, hung her head in deep

---

[1] Plumbariola (Piumarola) is a small town about 9 km from Cassino. Schuster notes, "A Cassinese tradition, whose origin is lost, places the *cella* of Scholastica at Plumbariola," although he then goes on to dispute the tradition. Other material from the tradition places her convent at Cassino. See Schuster, *St. Benedict and His Times*, 339.

sorrow and in a quiet and humble voice pleaded, "Oh Mother, it is impossible for me to do this thing, for my heart is burdened to the point of despair." And falling on her knees she begged Blessed Scholastica to listen to what it was that troubled her so deeply. Scholastica's countenance softened at the sight of Sinceria's distress, and she looked at her with motherly love. Taking the younger woman's hands in her own she said softly, "Speak, then, my child, for I am listening."

2. Sinceria, her eyes remaining fixed on Scholastica, continued with a modest and unassuming voice. She explained that her mother, a widow, who lived in Cassino, was dying, and that she was her only child. It would only be a short time now until her mother would close her eyes for the last time, and it was her deepest hope and prayer to be with her mother in her moment of departure. Indeed, it was her mother who had encouraged her to join Scholastica and the sisters when they first arrived in the town. She did this even though this departure of her daughter would leave her alone, such was her great wish to see her daughter's fervent desire to seek Christ fulfilled. Then, bowing her head in submission, Sinceria uttered these final words: "Even so dearest Mother—even after hearing the reasons for my plea—if you insist I do as you say, I will, with God's help, lovingly obey."[2]

3. After listening intently to Sinceria's story, the wise Scholastica sat for some time in silence as she pondered these things in her heart. And then she beckoned Sinceria to rise from her knees and dry her tears. In a firm but consoling voice she instructed Sinceria: "Return now to the

---

[2] See RB 68. The title of this chapter is "If a Brother Is Told to Do Impossible Tasks."

community, and I will follow shortly. We will find someone else to go to Plumbariola and minister with Fidelia and the other sisters. You will remain for the time being to care for your mother in her hour of need." Sinceria bowed humbly and asked Scholastica for a blessing, and then took her leave from the company of the holy twins.

4. Benedict, for his part, was amazed by this conversation between Scholastica and her young sister. "Sister, had we not just been speaking of the virtue of prompt, unhesitating obedience?" You may recall, Peter, the example of the virtue of this obedience from one of Benedict's own disciples.[3]

PETER: Oh yes, I remember it well. A wondrous story of the grace that one receives from such prompt adherence to obedience.

GREGORY: This is only too true, Peter. Nevertheless, listen to the deep wisdom that springs from charity in the words that Scholastica then uttered to her brother. "Did not Sinceria's distress and humble plea move you, brother? Did she not present her case patiently and without obstinacy? Was she not still willing to obey my command even though it would have brought great hardship, not only to her but to her dearly beloved and virtuous mother? Must we ask the impossible, brother—indeed the uncharitable and unholy— from those we serve as Christ in the community?"

Blessed Benedict was once again astounded by the depth of Scholastica's loving wisdom and exclaimed: "Truly, this warmest love which you have for your sisters has expanded your heart, my dearest sister. It is without doubt that your zealous love is that which leads to God and eternal life."[4]

---

[3] See *Dial.* II.VII.1-3 (33–34).
[4] See RB Prol. 49 and RB 72.

5. PETER: I am myself humbled by this tale of loving wisdom. It has indeed softened my heart.

GREGORY: For certain it softened holy Benedict's heart also, dear Peter, for he took this wisdom and applied it to his own love of the brothers in his community. This we find in the little Rule he wrote for his monks.[5] Now it is truly time for you to have your initial request fulfilled, which is to hear and understand the final conversation that ensued between this holy pair, who were filled with the light of God.

---

[5] See RB 68, "If a Brother Is Told to Do Impossible Tasks."

Chapter 18

The Final Meeting—
Holy Conversation

XVIII. 1 PETER: Having heard of this wondrous and charitable life of the Blessed Scholastica, I am now anxious and truly ready to hear of this last and holy conversation between the hallowed saints of God.[1]

GREGORY: Yes indeed, Peter. Your patience has been rewarded. For a long time, Blessed Scholastica had contemplated the love of God, not only in her prayer but in her untiring service of others both within and outside of her community. Indeed, she combined in herself both the active life of charity towards others from Martha and the contemplative life of leisure from Mary.[2] As she approached her final days, there was now only a longing to see the face of Love itself, and thus death held no terror for her gentle soul. The fire of divine love was so strong in her heart that she

---

[1] This life of Scholastica begins with Peter's desire to hear more of the contents of this final conversation. Gregory, however, insists that to understand this conversation, Peter must first hear all about the life of Scholastica.

[2] See Gregory the Great, *Moralia on Job*, Book VI, XXXVII:61, in Gregory the Great, *Moral Reflections on the Book of Job*, vol. 2 (87): "What is meant by Mary, who sits and listens to the Lord's words, but the contemplative life? What does Martha, who is occupied with external service, signify but the active life?"

had, indeed, come to that perfect love of God that casts out all fear.

2. Just as her brother, the holy man of God, Benedict, knew the moment of his death, so too did Scholastica know that her time was near. Indeed, she had a dream in which two bells that rang in sweet harmony for all to hear slowly merged to produce just one single tone, yet from this one bell emerged many smaller bells of wondrous variety in size, shape, color, and sound. These bells rang in a joyful and sweet cacophony of sound that, though an astonishing noise, was also a mysterious unifying force heralding a time of great unity in their immense diversity of form.

And so she informed her closest companions, the grace-filled Fidelia, Speranza, and Desideria, of her impending death, and sent a letter to her community at Plumbariola.

3. In preparation for this final moment of her spiritual journey, Scholastica desired to see her brother just one last time.

The circumstances of this meeting you already know, Peter. For on that most sublime night, as I have already related, Scholastica and Benedict spent many hours in holy converse concerning the joys of heaven. This meeting took place just before the beginning of Lent, and they talked of the unspeakable sweetness of love that rose in their hearts as they both looked forward to holy Easter with the joy of spiritual desire.[3] Heart to heart they revealed to each other what they had already experienced of these inexpressible delights of love here in this life.[4] Benedict found his own heart expanding further as Scholastica talked of meeting the face of Christ not only in her sisters but more especially in the poor, the lonely, the sick, the unloved, and the weary

[3] See RB 49.7.
[4] See RB Prol. 49.

traveler—and, indeed, of meeting the poor in the face of the wounded Christ in her prayers. It was here that she beheld the eyes of love longing to be loved.

4. Together they talked of the gentle and humble-hearted who see God in the ordinary events of daily life, in the common tasks of working and praying alongside their sisters and brothers in community; in the mother who gently sings her child to sleep with soft and gentle love songs; in the joy of the stranger who gives their coat to the cold beggar; in the kind word spoken to the angry, the reasonable word to the demanding, and the righteous word spoken in the face of injustice. They talked of their experience of the simple joy in the smile of the wounded who had been healed, of the friendship between enemies, and the quiet embrace of peace in the soul that gathers around those who are reconciled. They mused together on the wonders of creation, its pure gift of abundant variety which spoke of God's immense generosity. And, at last, they sat listening together in the silence of mystery—still . . . at peace— finally at rest in the love of God's embracing presence. Kissed with the kiss of Love itself. Beyond speech and lost in the eternal light that surrounded them in the darkness— at one in a moment of time. "What no eye has seen, nor ear heard, nor the human heart conceived," Scholastica and Benedict glimpsed together "what God has prepared for those who love him."[5] There, in this still moment, the sweet ringing of bells could be heard as the first rays of dawn rose over the crest of the mountain heralding a new day. And then they stood and together they began to sing their morning praises to God in full voice: "Oh that today you would listen to God's voice, harden not your hearts."[6]

---

[5] 1 Cor 2:9.
[6] See RB Prol. 10. This verse from Psalm 95 is traditionally used as the antiphon to the Invitatory Psalm (95) for the Vigil Office.

Chapter 19

Death of Scholastica

XIX. 1 Blessed Scholastica returned to her community with her companions later that day, and it was not long before she became very ill. Within a few days she called to her sisters to pray, for she knew that she was coming to the utmost limit of her earthly life,[1] and would soon join herself to Christ in her final act of consecration. She could see that her condition was of great distress to her sisters, and she soothed their heavy hearts with comforting and encouraging words: "We have lived our earthly lives faithfully together, my loving sisters, keeping death always before us as we look towards the joy of the resurrection[2] which is promised us in Christ Jesus. For death is merely a part of this journey we all must take to God in Christ. Do not be afraid therefore, but know for certain that perfect love casts out all fear, even the fear of death.[3] Know also that I place all my hope in God alone, as you do.[4] We have sought God together, and it is only with you all beside me in this my final journey that I have the courage to continue, as you

---

[1] See Gregory of Nyssa's words in *Life of Macrina* 24:1 (132).
[2] See RB 4.47 and 49.7.
[3] See RB 7.63.
[4] See RB 4.41.

must also do. My sisters, continue to let peace be your quest and aim and never despair of God's mercy."[5] Unafraid of what lay ahead of her, the holy one continued to impart deep wisdom to her sisters, concerning the joys of their life together, and in this way she showed forth the pure and divine love of Christ which she had nourished within her all her life.[6]

2. And then as the last evening rays of the sun shone through her open window, illuminating her face, she prayed over them:

> May you continue to practice that good zeal that separates us from evil and joins us to God in eternal life. With the warmest of love, be for each other and for your neighbor. Strive always to honor one another and bear with each other's frailty in both body and behavior with a Christ-like patience. Always lend a listening ear to each other, and in this way you will not simply pursue what you judge good for yourself but what is of most benefit for others as well. Show a selfless love for each other; in awe and wonder fear God out of the love from which you were made. With sincere and humble hearts love those who lead you in honesty. And may you prefer absolutely nothing to Christ, for indeed, he preferred nothing to us. And in his love may we all be led together to everlasting life.[7]

3. Surrounded by her beloved sisters, Scholastica slowly rose from her bed and stood with her arms raised to heaven, her face shining with a mysterious joy as, with the longing of a lover, she three times sang the following verse from the

---

[5] See RB Prol. 17 and 4.74.

[6] See *Life of Macrina* 24:2 (132).

[7] This section of Scholastica's instruction and prayer is basically a paraphrase of RB 72.

Psalms: *Suscipe me, Domine, secundum eloquium tuum, et vivam et non confundas me ab expectatione mea.* "Receive me, Lord, as you have promised, and I will live. Do not disappoint me in my hope."[8] Then she reclined once more and looked gently and lovingly at the sisters as they all joined in her chant with:

> *Gloria Patri, et Filio, et Spiritui Sancto,*
> *Sicut erat in principio, et nunc, et semper, et in sæcula*
>   *sæculorum. Amen.*
> (Glory to the Father, and to the Son, and to the Holy Spirit,
> As it was in the beginning, is now, and ever shall be, world
>   without end. Amen.)

4. As Scholastica finally closed her eyes and gave up her spirit the room became full of the fragrance of honeysuckle and lemon. Her face appeared to shine with a glorious light as if there was no darkness in the room at all, but only a golden light permeating the air and spreading over all those present with its glow. Though the sisters wept while keeping vigil with her body throughout the next three days, with their chapel bell tolling its sorrow, there was no abating of the sweet smell emanating from around Scholastica's holy body.

---

[8] RB 58.21, Ps 118(119):116.

Chapter 20

Burial of Scholastica and Benedict

XX. 1 PETER: My heart is truly stirred by this account, and there are tears welling in my eyes, but I recall from our previous conversation that these blessed siblings were not separated in body by the grave, so united were they in heart and mind in life, even as you say, from the beginning.[1]

GREGORY: Your memory serves you well, Peter. They were united in birth, united in mind and heart in their way of seeking God, and they were indeed united in death. And as Scholastica was the first to come forth into this life, so she was the first to leave it. You may also remember well that Benedict himself had a vision of Scholastica, three days after her death, where he saw her soul, in the likeness of a dove, received into the heavenly places.[2] For he knew in the depth of his heart that his holy sister was united with God, and longed to be with her in such unspeakable delight of love and mystery.

2. Thus it occurred that Benedict sent his dearest disciples, Maurus and Placid, under obedience, to obtain the body of holy Scholastica. The sisters were of course initially reluctant to hand their beloved Mother over to the holy

[1] See *Dial.* II.XXXIV.2 (125).
[2] See *Dial.* II.XXXIV.1 (125).

monks, but it was Desideria, who had been particularly close to Scholastica during her earthly life, who revealed to them that Scholastica had herself expressed her desire to be united with her brother in the grave. So they carefully laid her body on a bier, adorned with many herbs and flowers. Placing a parchment of the Scriptures on her breast and a simple wooden cross in her hands, they knelt in prayer as the two brothers began to softly chant their own farewell:

> *Nunc dimittis servum tuum, Domine, secundum verbum*
>   *tuum in pace:*
> *Quia viderunt oculi mei salutare tuum*
> *Quod parasti ante faciem omnium populorum:*
> *Lumen ad revelationem gentium, et gloriam plebis tuae*
>   *Israel.*
> (Master, now you are dismissing your servant in peace,
>   according to your word;
> for my eyes have seen your salvation,
>   which you have prepared in the presence of all peoples,
> a light for revelation to the Gentiles
>   and for glory to your people Israel.[3])

3. Then Placid and Maurus lifted the bier, and with Fidelia, Speranza, and Desideria carried Scholastica up the mountain. As the church bells rang across the valley, many came with candles to help escort her remains in this solemn procession to the monastery of holy Benedict, where he reccived her into their chapel as the monks continued to chant psalms of praise and thanksgiving. And not long after, as you know, Peter, the holy man of God, after receiving a vision and anticipating his own departure, joined his blessed sister in the heavenly realms.[4]

---

[3] The *Nunc Dimittis*, or the "Canticle of Simeon," is the canticle sung at Compline (Night Prayer) in Benedictine communities. It is taken from Luke 2:29-32.

[4] See *Dial.* II.XXXV.3 (132) and XXXVII.1 (139).

Postscript

PETER: I am deeply moved by these final stories of the blessed Scholastica and her death. Though I sense a sadness in her dying, my heart is also filled to overflowing with an unexpected wonder and ecstasy.

GREGORY: The holy woman's life was ordered and disciplined in such a way as to obtain this cherished goal of heaven, Peter. Yet is it not true that we are material beings, born of flesh? If we are not believers, then we can come to doubt that anything exists beyond what we can see with our own bodily eyes. But as believers we know, through both reason and faith, that our souls live on after death, and thus we sense a mixture of both sadness and joy at the death of a loved one.[1] Only spiritual death brings us fear and dread, Peter, not bodily death.[2] And so it is reasonable to say that we must limit our grief, for it would indicate our lack of hope and doubt in the eternal life of the soul should an over-abundance of tears flow.[3]

---

[1] See *Dial.* IV.1.2 (91).

[2] See Gregory the Great, *Moralia on Job*, Book XI, XVII:26, in *Moral Reflections on the Book of Job*, vol. 3: Books 11–16, trans Brian Keius, Cistercian Studies 258 (Collegeville, MN: Cistercian Publications, 2016), 25.

[3] See Gregory the Great's letter 9.220 to Aregius, bishop in Gaul, in *The Letters of Gregory the Great*, vol. 2, trans. John R. C. Martyn (Toronto: Pontifical Institute of Mediaeval Studies, 2004), 668–90.

We now know that Benedict and Scholastica, whose bodies rest in the one place, continue to watch over those who seek God's wisdom and their intercession. Their lives on this earth rang with the sweet harmony of God's love for all those whom they met, and with this same harmony they now sing God's praises in the glory of God's loving presence with all the saints. The little plant that they sowed in the fertile soil of this land continues to grow into a noble tree even in our own time, Peter.[4]

PETER: What you have told me is of great benefit to my soul and has left me greatly edified.

GREGORY: And now we must cease from our conversation and spend some time with the still silence of our hearts as we ponder on all we have heard of the workings of God's grace in the lives of these great saints. Let us pray, in union with them, that peace may come to our troubled world as we strive to love God and our neighbor with all our hearts, with all our minds, and with all our strength.

---

[4] This phrase is drawn from an 1870 pastoral letter of John Bede Polding. See *The Eye of Faith: The Pastoral Letters of John Bede Polding*, ed. Gregory Haines, Mary Gregory Forster, and Frank Brophy (Kilmore, Vic: Lowden Publishing, 1978), 335.

Acknowledgments

This little book had its beginnings while I was on sabbatical at the Collegeville Institute, Minnesota, in 2017. I am grateful to Don Ottenhoff, the former executive director of the Institute, who encouraged me to pursue my idea for creating a hagiography of St. Scholastica. I was also inspired by the work of the other scholars at the Institute at the time, especially Daphne Haywood, Arland Jacobson, and Jean Flannelly. Their friendship, conversation, and deep wisdom sustained me, and their solid commitment to their projects kept me focused on my own work.

That initial work lay dormant for some time until my colleagues at the Yarra Theology Union (a member College of the University of Divinity, Melbourne), Claire Renkin and Janette Bredenoord Elliott, co-opted me into their plans to present a session of three papers for the Leeds International Medieval Conference in 2022. Their heartfelt optimism in my project helped me believe that Scholastica's story was not only a critical addition to the hagiographical record but also a valuable work of promoting the missing voices of women from monastic and church history.

I am indebted to Michael Casey for making time amid his own hectic writing schedule to contribute a foreword to my work, and to Matthew Beckmann, who has translated the two medieval lives of Scholastica that I needed to complete my research.

Finally, I am lovingly grateful to my community, particularly Jill O'Brien and Donna Belle Ferrer, who both helped bear the burden of my writing—patiently listening to my struggles to articulate my ideas—and were unwearied from reading my manuscript. Their constant companionship, critique, and belief in my project have been both inspirational and invaluable.

Bibliography

Primary Sources

The Acts of Paul and Thecla. Translated by Jeremiah Jones. Kerry, Ireland: CrossReach Publications, 2019.

Aelred of Rievaulx. *Spiritual Friendship*. Translated by Lawrence C. Braceland. Edited by Marsha L. Dutton. Cistercian Fathers 5. Collegeville, MN: Cistercian Publications, 2010.

Alberic of Cassino. *The Life of St Scholastica*. In Dom Anselmo Lentini, "L'omilia e la vita di S. Scolastica di Alberic Cassinese." *Benedictina* 3 (1949): 217–38.

Athanasius. *The Life of Antony and the Letter to Marcellinus*. Translated by Robert C. Gregg. New York: Paulist Press, 1980.

Augustine. *Augustine of Hippo and His Monastic Rule*. Translated by George Lawless. Oxford: Clarendon, 1987.

Augustine. *The Works of Saint Augustine: A Translation for the 21st Century: Sermons*. Vol. 4. Translated by Edmund Hill. Brooklyn, NY: New City Press, 1992.

Egeria: Diary of a Pilgrimage. Translated by George E. Gingras. Ancient Christian Writers, No. 38. New York: Paulist Press, 1970.

Gregory of Nyssa. *The Life of Macrina*. In *Macrina the Younger, Philosopher of God*, 109–48. Translated by Anna M. Silvas. Medieval Women–Texts and Contexts. Turnhout, Belgium: Brepols, 2008.

Gregory the Great. *Forty Gospel Homilies*. Translated by David Hurst. Cistercian Studies 123. Collegeville, MN: Cistercian Publications, 1990.

Gregory the Great. *Homilies of Saint Gregory the Great on the Book of the Prophet Ezekiel*. Translated by Theodosia Gray. Etna, CA: Center for Traditionalist Orthodox Studies, 1990.

Gregory the Great. *The Letters of Gregory the Great*. Vols. 1 and 2. Translated by John R. C. Martyn. Toronto: Pontifical Institute of Mediaeval Studies, 2004.

Gregory the Great. *The Life of Saint Benedict*. Commentary by Adalbert de Vogüé. Translated by Hilary Costello and Eoin de Bhaldraithe. Petersham, MA: St. Bede's Publications, 1993.

Gregory the Great. *The Life of St. Benedict by Gregory the Great*. Translated by Terrence G. Kardong. Collegeville, MN: Liturgical Press, 2009.

Gregory the Great. *Moral Reflections on the Book of Job*. Vol. 2: Books 6–10. Translated by Brian Kerns. Cistercian Studies 257. Collegeville, MN: Cistercian Publications, 2015.

Gregory the Great. *Moral Reflections on the Book of Job*. Vol. 3: Books 11–16. Translated by Brian Kerns. Cistercian Studies 258. Collegeville, MN: Cistercian Publications, 2016.

Gregory the Great. *Pastoral Care (Regulae Pastoralis)*. Translated by Henry Davis. Ancient Christian Writers, No. 11. New York: Newman Press, 1950/1978.

Gregory the Great. *Saint Gregory the Great: Dialogues on the Miracles of the Italian Fathers*. The Fathers of the Church, Vol. 39. Translated by Odo John Zimmerman. New York: Ex Fontibus, 2016.

John Bede Polding. *The Eye of Faith: The Pastoral Letters of John Bede Polding*. Edited by Gregory Haines, Mary Gregory Forster, and Frank Brophy. Kilmore, Vic: Lowden Publishing, 1978.

John Cassian. *John Cassian: The Conferences*. Translated by Boniface Ramsey. Ancient Christian Writers, No. 57. New York: Newman Press, 1997.

Kardong, Terrence G. *Benedict's Rule: A Translation and Commentary*. Collegeville, MN: Liturgical Press, 2021.

The Life of St. Brigit the Virgin by Cogitosus. In *Celtic Spirituality*. Translated by Oliver Davies, 122–39. New York: Paulist Press, 1999.

The Life of St Radegunde by the Nun, Baudonivia. In *Handmaids of the Lord: Holy Women in Late Antiquity and the Early Middle Ages*. Translated by Joan M. Petersen, 401–24. Cistercian Studies 143. Collegeville, MN: Cistercian Publications, 1996.

Palladius of Aspuna. *The Lausiac History*. Translated by John Wortley. Cistercian Studies 252. Collegeville, MN: Cistercian Publications, 2015.

Petri Diaconi. *De Viris Illustribus Casinensis Coenobii*. Patrologiae Cursus Completus. Series Latina 173. Edited by J.-P. Migne. Paris: Garnier, 1895.

Procopius. *The Anecdota or Secret History*. Vol. 6. Translated by Henry Bronson Dewing. Loeb Classical Library. Cambridge, MA: Harvard University Press, 1960.

"Pseudo-Athanasius: The Life and Activity of the Holy and Blessed Teacher Syncletica." Translated by Elizabeth A. Castelli. In *Ascetic Behavior in Greco-Roman Antiquity: A Sourcebook*, edited by Vincent L. Wimbush, 265–311. Minneapolis: Fortress Press, 1990.

Pseudo-Athanasius. *The Life and Regimen of the Blessed and Holy Syncletica; Part One: The Translation*. Translated by Elizabeth Bryson Bongie. Eugene, OR: Wipf and Stock, 2005; Toronto: Peregrina, 2003.

RB 1980: The Rule of St. Benedict in Latin and English with Notes. Edited by Timothy Fry, Imogene Baker, Timothy Horner, Augusta Raabe, and Mark Sheridan. Collegeville, MN: Liturgical Press, 1981.

Rudolf, Monk of Fulda. *The Life of Saint Leoba*. In *The Anglo-Saxon Missionaries in Germany: Being the Lives of SS. Willibrord, Boniface, Sturm, Leoba, and Lebuin, Together with the Hodoeporicon of St. Willibald and a Selection from the Correspondence of St. Boniface*. Translated by Charles H. Talbot, 205–26. New York: Sheed and Ward, 1954.

The Rule of St Basil in Latin and English: A Revised Critical Edition. Translated by Anna M. Silvas. Collegeville, MN: Liturgical Press, 2013.

The Sayings of the Desert Fathers: The Alphabetical Collection. Translated by Benedicta Ward. Cistercian Studies 59. Collegeville, MN: Cistercian Publications, 1975.

Willibald. *The Life of St. Boniface*. In *The Anglo-Saxon Missionaries in Germany: Being the Lives of SS. Willibrord, Boniface, Sturm, Leoba, and Lebuin, Together with the Hodoeporicon of St. Willibald and a Selection from the Correspondence of St. Boniface*. Translated by Charles H. Talbot, 25–62. New York: Sheed and Ward, 1954.

Secondary Sources

Alpern, Sara, Joyce Antler, Elisabeth Israels Perry, and Ingrid Winther Scobie, eds. "Introduction." In *The Challenge of Feminist Biography: Writing the Lives of Modern American Women*, 1–15. Urbana: University of Illinois Press, 1992.

Boo, Mary Richard, and Joan M. Braun. "Emerging from the Shadows: St. Scholastica." In *Medieval Women Monastics: Wisdom's Wellsprings*, edited by Miriam Schmitt and Linda Kulzer, 1–11. Collegeville, MN: Liturgical Press, 1996.

Dalladay, Jill. *The Abbess of Whitby: A Novel of Hild of Northumbria*. Oxford: Lion Fiction, 2015.

Drobner, Hubertus R. *The Fathers of the Church: A Comprehensive Introduction.* Peabody, MA: Hendrickson, 2007.

Gaarder, Jostein. *Vita Brevis: A Letter to St Augustine.* Translated by Anne Born. London: Phoenix, 1997.

Gooder, Paula. *Lydia: A Story.* London: Hodder & Stoughton, 2022.

Gooder, Paula. *Phoebe: A Story.* London: Hodder & Stoughton, 2018.

Gooder, Paula. "Phoebe: A Talk by Paula Gooder." Recorded live at St Ann with Emmauel Church, Nottingham, September 22, 2019. https://www.youtube.com/watch?v=tsBrJLjb_xQ&t=2951s.

Harper, Kyle. *The Fate of Rome: Climate, Disease, and the End of an Empire.* Princeton: Princeton University Press, 2017.

Heather, Peter. *Rome Resurgent: War and Empire in the Age of Justinian.* Oxford: Oxford University Press, 2018.

Heffernan, Thomas J. *Sacred Biography: Saints and Their Biographers in the Middle Ages.* New York: Oxford University Press, 1988.

Kardong, Terrence G. *Benedict Backwards: Reading the Rule in the Twenty-First Century.* Collegeville, MN: Liturgical Press, 2017.

Krusch, Bruno. "Zur Florians- und Lupus-Legende. Eine Entgegnung (Fortsetzung)." *Neues Archiv der Gesellschaft für ältere deutsche Geschichtskunde* 24 (1899): 533–70.

Leccisotti, Tommaso. *Monte Cassino.* Translated by Armand O. Citarella. Abbey of Monte Cassino, 1987.

Leclercq, Jean. *The Love of Learning and the Desire for God: A Study of Monastic Culture.* Translated by Catharine Misrahi. New York: Fordham University Press, 1982.

Markus, R. A. *Gregory the Great and His World.* Cambridge: Cambridge University Press, 1997.

Mayeski, Marie Anne. "Baudonivia's Life of St. Radegunde: A Theology of Power." In *Women at the Table: Three Medieval Theologians,* 105–47. Collegeville, MN: Liturgical Press, 2004.

Meyvaert, Paul. "The Historical Setting and Significance of the *Codex Benedictus.*" *Codex Benedictus (Vat. Lat. 1202). An Eleventh Century Lectionary from Monte Cassino.* New York and Zurich: Johnson Reprint Corporation, 1981, 1982.

Morin, Germain. "Les quatre anciens calendriers du Mont-Cassin (VIIIe et IXe siècles)." *Revue Bénédictine* 25 (1908).

Palmer, James T. *Early Medieval Hagiography.* Leeds, UK: Arc Humanities Press, 2018.

Petersen, Joan M. *Handmaids of the Lord: Holy Women in Late Antiquity and the Early Middle Ages*. Cistercian Studies 143. Collegeville, MN: Cistercian Publications, 1996.

Schmitt, Miriam, and Linda Kulzer, eds. *Medieval Women Monastics: Wisdom's Wellsprings*. Collegeville, MN: Liturgical Press, 1996.

Schuster, Ildefonso. *St. Benedict and His Times*. Translated by Gregory J. Roettger. St. Louis: Herder, 1951.

Seewald, Peter. *Benedict XVI: A Life*, Vol. 1, *Youth in Nazi Germany to the Second Vatican Council 1927–1965*. Translated by Dinah Livingstone. London: Bloomsbury Continuum, 2020; Vol. 2, *Professor and Prefect to Pope and Pope Emeritus 1966–Present*. Translated by Dinah Livingstone. London: Bloomsbury Continuum, 2021.

Valeri, Biancamaria. *Ferentino sfumature di luce e storia*. Rome: Dantebus Edizioni, 2022.

Vivian, Tim. "Courageous Women: Three Desert Ammas—Theodora, Sarah, and Syncletica; A New Translation from the Greek Alphabetical Apophthegmata Patrum, with Introduction, Notes, and Comments." *American Benedictine Review* 71, no. 1 (2020): 75–107.

Wacker, Grant. "Promises (and Perils) of the 'New Hagiography.'" *Fides et Historia* 49, no. 2 (2017): 45–48.

Ward, Benedicta. *Harlots of the Desert: A Study of Repentance in Early Monastic Sources*. Collegeville, MN: Cistercian Publications, 1987.